Running Your Own Pub

running your own PUB

Elven Money

**THE
KOGAN PAGE**
Working for Yourself
SERIES

Acknowledgements

Thank you Mike Barnett, Roger Brown, Johnny Morrice and Ralph Nelson for your invaluable help and advice. Credit and gratitude are due to Jackie. Among those who will not be forgotten for their friendship and inspiration, and for their part in forming my experience in the trade, I would mention my mother, Tony and Wendy, Ella and Stanley, all my favourite pubs and the staff and customers of the Plough, the Eight Bells, and the Tally Ho. Nothing can repay Sam for her encouragement, perceptive criticism, and unflagging labour.

Elven Money
August 1984

Copyright © Elven Money 1985

All rights reserved

First published in Great Britain in 1985
by Kogan Page Limited
120 Pentonville Road
London N1 9JN
Reprinted 1985, 1986

British Library Cataloguing in Publication Data

Money, Elven
  Running your own pub.
  1. Hotel management—Great Britain
  I. Title
  647′.95′068   TX911.3.M27

  ISBN 0 85038 927 5 Hb
  ISBN 0 85038 928 3 Pb

Printed in Great Britain by
Biddles Ltd, Guildford

Contents

Introduction   7
Author's note 11

1. What is a Pub?   12
Why do people go to a pub? 13; Your
personality 14; Professionalism 16; Basic
policy 18; The secret of success 19

2. Finding Your Pub   20
Entry into the trade 20; Professional
advice 24; Organising the search 25; What to
look out for 27; Potential profitability 30;
Raising the finance 31; Negotiating a
tenancy 39; Purchasing a free house 41;
Change-over day 42

3. The Customer   46
The customer's wants and needs 46; Customer
relations 48; Undesirable custom 51

4. The Pub and How to 'Sell' It   54
Advertising 54; Publicity 56; Outside
appearance 57; Inside appearance 60

5. Drink   77
Beer 78; Spirits 83; Wine 85; Cocktails 87;
Soft drinks 88; Cigarettes and tobacco 88;
Marketing 89; Buying 90; Equipment 92

6. Food   94
Market research 95; Supplies 95; Portions 96;
Menu 97; Service 100; Equipment 102;
Hygiene 103

7. Finance and Accounting 105
The accounts 105; Value added tax 112;
Wages 112; Insurance 113; Office
organisation 114

8. Staff 115
Engagement 115; Training 117;
Supervision 118; Delegation 119;
Dismissal 120

9. Pub-keeping and the Law 122
Police 122; Licence 123; Alterations 128;
Children 128; Drunkenness 129; Betting,
gaming and lotteries 129; Amusement
machines 130; Race relations and sex
discrimination 130; Liquid measures 130;
Dilution and adulteration 131;
Copyright 131; Credit 131

10. Daily Operation of the Pub 132
Daily organisation 132; Paperwork 133;
Cleaning 133; Bottling up 135; Cellar
work 135; Food preparation 136; Odds
and ends 136; Opening time 137; Closing
time 137; Evening session 138

11. Time Off 140
Staff 141; Which day? 141; Getting
away 142; Holidays 142; Personal life 143

12. The Future 145
Strategy 145; Ideas for expansion 149;
Success 152

Appendix 153
Books 153; Journals 153; Courses 154;
Useful addresses 154

Index 156

Introduction

The landlord of the local where I first learned to pull a pint often declared that he had previously spent so much time in front of the bar that he decided he might as well buy the pub, move to the other side of the counter, and turn his expense into profit. His customers were pleased he made the switch. He ran a first-class establishment.

However, I am sure his reasons for taking such a drastic step were somewhat more profound than he suggested. For it *is* a drastic step. Starting any business demands a dramatic change in your way of life. Taking on a pub necessitates a total revolution.

Keeping a pub is like no other business. It requires complete dedication—thinking, living, breathing *pub*, 24 hours a day. Even on your day off you will probably find yourself in somebody else's pub, watching how they do things, and wondering about what is happening back home.

But at the same time it has very special rewards. There is immense satisfaction in creating a comfortable, cheerful, enticing environment, and in providing drinks and food which you are confident are of a high standard. There is great pleasure in watching your customers enjoying themselves, and in hearing them confirm it with their, 'Thank you, landlord' as they leave. There is the sheer fun of presiding over a busy evening in your own pub; the chatter, the laughter, the good-humoured banter, the warm and companionable atmosphere. Not a bad way to earn a living!

So, it is time to take stock. The fact that you are considering such a step at all suggests that you are not entirely happy with your present situation. Something is missing. There seems to be a want of

Running Your Own Pub

satisfaction, of challenge. Life somehow lacks that spark.

This is good. This is the spur to progress. If you were satisfied you would have no need to improve your lot. But is the spur strong enough? Is your dissatisfaction so urgent that you really want to face the challenge of the unknown?

This is one of the most important decisions of your life, which will have far-reaching effects on you and your family for years to come. It is also the first of a multitude of decisions you will have to take while setting up your business, and during the day-to-day running of it. It is essential to tackle it properly, here and now. If you are not ready to take the decision, then you are not ready to take a pub.

Write down a list of all the benefits of your present way of life. Perhaps you have a secure job, a regular pay cheque, reasonable working hours, paid holidays, a good pension to look forward to; you and your family have built up a comfortable home, you have satisfying hobbies and a circle of friends who share your interests; and so on.

Now make a list of the drawbacks of your situation. Possibly you find your job monotonous, noisy and dirty. You have no real responsibility, and can see little chance of progress in the long years before collecting your pension. Your talents are unappreciated and under-used. Perhaps your leisure time seems increasingly to be spent in front of the telly, watching the umpteenth game of snooker, while an uneasy, nagging feeling tells you that life has more to offer than this.

Of course, you may be unemployed, you may have been made redundant, or you may have just retired from the services, in which case your list will look very different. Try to get down everything that is at all relevant, and then give each point serious consideration. Be quite sure that it really is an important aspect of your present way of life, or whether you merely accept that it is because everyone else seems to think so.

Now write down all the benefits and drawbacks of running a pub. I can help a bit here with a few

8

suggestions but, once again, you must bring your own ideas to bear.

Benefits:
Your own boss.
Responsible for your own future.
An important and satisfying job, providing a service to the community.
An interesting and enjoyable occupation.
Prestige and popularity.
Companionship.
Pleasant working conditions.
No travelling to work.
You choose your place of work, and working conditions.

Drawbacks:
As the boss you have no higher authority to turn to for a decision—it's *your* problem.
Long working hours—70 to 80 per week.
No weekends or bank holidays off.
No holidays at first, and difficult to organise and pay for when you feel you can take them.
Leisure activities severely curtailed.
You live on top of the job.
Little time to devote to your children.
Occasional unpleasant decisions, eg, sacking employees, barring customers.
The law tends to be on the employees' side. You are now the employer.

You will notice that I have made very little mention of financial benefits. This is because, although money, at the end of the day, is what business is all about, it must not be the reason for changing your way of life. During the early years, when you are working your hardest, there will be precious little money about, and what there is you will want to plough back into the business. It will be your enthusiasm that will carry you through, not the immediate financial rewards.

You must also take a long, hard look at yourself, and, if there is to be one, your partner. If your partner is, in addition, your husband or wife, there is an important personal, as well as business, relationship to consider. Make no mistake, running a pub will have profound effects on your character, and therefore on any relationship you may have. Look at yourself with honesty. Evaluate your personality. Be sure you are the right person for the job.

Certain basic characteristics can be considered to be essential:

Determination. The ability to keep going; to be there at opening time, a cheerful, friendly host when, behind the scenes, everything is in a state of chaos; to persevere, overcoming all obstacles, until your goal is achieved.

Enthusiasm. If you are not enthusiastic about your business, nobody else will be.

Adaptability. Being prepared to adjust to new circumstances, and consider alternative ways of achieving your aims. It is also a most useful virtue when dealing with an unending variety of customers.

Sociability. Pretty obvious this one, but it is amazing how many landlords have not got it. And remember, it means the ability to get on with *all* types, classes, and ages of people, even those that irritate you.

Good humour. A great asset. It not only helps to overcome obstacles, but also ensures a smiling face behind the bar.

Patience. You will need unending patience when dealing with staff, suppliers, representatives, and of course your customers—they pay your wages.

Good health. You will be working hard, both physically and mentally, between 14 and 16 hours a day, six or seven days a week. This job has no paid sick leave, and you cannot afford long periods away from the driver's seat. Be sure of your ability to withstand the physical strain and mental stress. Have a thorough check up if you have any doubts.

Give all these points a thorough going over. Thrash them out with your partner. Approach this first decision of your new business life in a professional manner.

If a careful decision has left you still raring to go, still eager to enter a world of hard work, challenge and excitement, then read on. Discover how to harness your enthusiasm to your new enterprise and achieve success.

Author's note

Throughout this book I have used such words as 'landlord' and 'he', and have not made any concessions to the prevailing, and most inconvenient fashion for constantly mentioning both sexes. This is not, however, founded on any chauvinistic opinions. On the contrary I would earnestly encourage women to seriously consider taking a pub. There are far too many women in a largely unappreciated, behind-the-scenes supportive role in the licensed trade, instead of 'up front'. I believe that many women are particularly suited to a profession that, at bottom, requires a caring approach.

There are a few highly successful landladies in their own right, and I can see no reason for any objection to many more which is not founded in prejudice, and perhaps in a fear of their possibly greater abilities.

I feel sure that the active encouragement of women to enter the business will have nothing but beneficial effects on the standards of public houses in this country, and I call upon the trade to adopt more enlightened attitudes.

Chapter 1
What is a Pub?

You will doubtless consider that you know the answer to this question very well. In fact you will probably have spent many happy hours finding out!

The obvious answer is that it is a place that sells alcoholic drinks, and often food, to be consumed on the premises; a simple retail organisation, exchanging goods for cash. Just like any shop, it is merely a matter of providing the right merchandise, at the right price, in an efficient manner.

I often get the impression that many, if not most, landlords go into the trade with just this idea. All you have to do is stock the shelves, fix a competitive price, and sit back to wait for the customers to flock in.

And so often this is literally what you see. The landlord *sitting* on a stool behind the bar, feeling disgruntled because people go in their hundreds to the pub down the road while his is empty. It does not occur to him that it might be his fault. He blames the brewer, the economic situation, the weather, the government: anything rather than himself.

His irritation is increased by the fact that he has to get off the stool to serve you. You want ice? Then you have to hang on while he goes round the back to get it. Another trip is necessary to get a lemon. The white wine is warm because he hasn't got round to putting it in the fridge.

The landlord then either totally ignores you, or bashes your ear with his troubles and his bewilderment at the lack of trade. When you get the chance, you look around the pub, and quickly realise some of the other reasons why he has few customers. The whole place has come to reflect the negative attitude that he has developed towards his business. He sees

12

no point in making a welcome for customers that do not come, and all the little touches, all the little extra tasks that might spring from enthusiasm, are neglected. As a result the pub is dreary, dirty, cold and dark.

Why do people go to a pub?

No, it is not a simple retail organisation. Furthermore, it is like no other business in the world. The pub trade is unique, and to be successful in it you need to understand why. Hence my question 'What is a pub?' which I am going to answer by asking a further question, 'Why do people go to a pub?'

The answer surely is obvious — 'For a drink'. But if this were the answer, and if a pub was a straightforward retail organisation, then everybody would go to the supermarket where liquor is very much cheaper, and drink in the warmth and comfort of their own homes in front of the telly. No worries about the breathalyser, and a quick, easy stagger up to bed at the end of the evening.

We need a place where life is as it should be. Where the landlord recognises us, is actually pleased to see us, addresses us by name, asks after our health, and wants to know how he can serve us. He doesn't care about our social standing—to him we are all VIPs. We begin to feel human again, to see ourselves as individuals who matter.

Friends there buy us a drink, sympathise with our problems, listen to and respect our opinions, perhaps even laugh at our jokes. They don't nag us, boss us or threaten us. With the help of a pint we soon relax. We soon become friendly, sociable beings who are keen to help and appreciate others. We pass around the cigarettes, stand our round, offer to help a mate fix his car, paint his house, mend his lawn-mower. We chat, we laugh, we feel for a while that all's right with the world.

In short, people go to a pub to experience a marvellous (and unique) atmosphere, which shuts out the nasty 'real' world, boosts their self-esteem, and brings out the nicer side of their natures. It brings them into contact with friends, and other interesting people, in comfortable surroundings over a satisfying, relaxing drink.

Notice that drink is just one part of the picture: the lubricant, if you like, which smoothes the way to enjoyment. Of course, it is the avowed reason for a visit to the pub, and indeed for the very existence of that establishment. But at the end of the day, what you, the publican, are selling is not just 'booze'.

To answer my question then, people go to a pub to find companionship, an ego boost, relaxation, enjoyment, a cosy environment away from the pressures of a workaday world. In other words, they go to find an 'atmosphere', a total ambience, conducive to their emotional and psychological well-being.

A pub provides that atmosphere in a way that no other place does. It also provides drink and food, but if this was its basic purpose it would soon succumb to the supermarket and the restaurant. This is what makes this trade unique, and turns it into a way of life full of excitement and challenge.

All you need is common sense and hard work. As long as you understand that it, and not the booze, is the basis of your business, then your decisions and actions will logically follow on, and the drinks will almost sell themselves.

Your personality

The first logical follow-on is to take a look at your own personality. To a large extent the landlord *is* the pub. His personality will be reflected in everything about the place. If he is a miserable old codger, it will be a miserable old pub. It will be cold because he is too mean and too lazy to light a fire. It will be uncomfortable because he is too selfish and uncaring to worry about his customers' needs. It will be dreary because his meanness of spirit will be reflected in the decor and furnishings.

Of course, we all have different personalities. The last thing I am suggesting is that all landlords become automatons with fixed smiles and a subservient demeanour. What is needed is a critical self-

What is a Pub?

examination to winkle out and get rid of negative attitudes, and to discover positive ones which can be encouraged and enhanced. Try to be aware of these attitudes as you talk to, and deal with, people in everyday life. Instead of looking for ways to get out of doing things for others, find out how you can help them. Instead of trying to prove how superior *you* are, try to show just how much you admire *them*. Instead of saying 'no', cultivate the habit of saying 'yes'.

I received a letter from some hardly-known relatives: 'We are thinking of taking a pub. Can we come to stay with you for a few months to learn the trade?' My first reaction was negative. I was quite busy enough without hangers-on, getting in the way, disrupting my private life as well as my business, constantly asking questions. However, a sense of family obligation and the glimmerings of a more positive attitude changed my mind. They stayed six months, turned out to be charming companions, great fun to be with, and a tremendous help in the pub. They even took over the running of the place while I had two glorious weeks' holiday. Not for one instant did I regret saying 'yes'.

It is a constant surprise how easy it is to say 'yes'; how often a receptive response, a willingness to please, brings its own rewards. When you are behind the bar it is of paramount importance.

For example, when a customer walks into your pub you might think, 'Good Lord, here comes old Fred. I can't stand another evening of his chatter.' The positive approach would be, 'How can I make sure that old Fred feels welcome, wanted, comfortable and happy?'

Because, you see, 'old Fred', and everyone else who is treated in the same positive way, will be in no hurry to give up their temporary bit of comfort and happiness, and will more than likely stay on for a few more pints. What is even more important, they will want to return again and again to rediscover that pleasant feeling—and fill your till.

Foreigners are often, for some reason, disliked and discouraged by publicans, more especially as they often expect table service, are not used to paying immediately for their drinks, and are completely non-plussed by our licensing laws. A little bit of give and take, a willingness to help and be welcoming, can overcome these problems and lead to a pleasant and profitable interlude.

One group of young people were, unknown to me, from an English language school which had just opened nearby. By treating them well as a matter of course I got the unexpected bonus of their recommendation, which brought a constant flow of big-spending students for years afterwards.

Remember, this is a business, and it is your *job* to be a cheerful, welcoming person. Be miserable and you will soon have falling profits to be miserable about. Be cheerful and you will keep laughing all the way to the bank. What is more, a cheerful landlord is a popular landlord, and so he earns a double bonus. We are all vain enough to enjoy being popular, and there is nothing wrong with that, but at the same time his popularity brings in the money. Make sure you earn that popularity and you will automatically earn the cash.

However, being a cheerful landlord does not mean that you have to be a one-man cabaret, entertaining your customers with your unrivalled wit, your fascinating tales, or your profound knowledge on many subjects. There is perhaps a place for all these things, but your job is much more to be the enthralled audience while your customer tells the jokes, gives you the benefit of his wisdom, or unburdens his troubled soul.

Professionalism

What all this boils down to is the cultivation within yourself of a professional approach to your business. Fortunately for you, if you do this, you are already ahead of much of the competition, for professionalism is, at present, often sadly lacking in the licensed trade. The popular idea of the genial host, who seems so relaxed and easygoing, has led to a widely held belief among budding publicans as well as the general public, that pub-keeping is more a hobby than a proper job.

A gentleman once approached me with a view to buying my pub. He had his own business to run, but his wife was bored at home all day. He just wanted something to keep her occupied!

Like many others, he thought that all the publican has to do is spend a few hours a day leaning on the bar, quaffing the drinks that the customers have bought him, and swapping jokes and reminiscences in most pleasant surroundings. At closing time, of course, he is only too glad to get rid of the customers so that he can put his feet up with a large glass of scotch while he plans his next Caribbean holiday and chats up that rather friendly young lady who works for him.

This attitude dies hard and quickly brings the more starry-eyed newcomer to the trade to the sort of disillusionment discussed earlier. For he believes that the public are simply there to bring him money in exchange for pints of beer, and when they stop doing that it must be their fault. He has not understood that *he* is the prime mover, and *he* must take the action that will result in the prosperity of his business. He has no one to blame but himself.

I believe that the major skill required in pub-keeping, and possibly the most difficult, is to promote the feeling of cosy, easygoing informality in the bar, while at the same time remembering that you are running a business, and one that is a lot harder and more demanding than most. The atmosphere which brings the customers in relies, not only on the cheerful, outgoing side of the landlord's personality, but also on his hard-headed, businesslike approach to the behind-the-scenes organisation.

Unseen and unrealised by the customer you must run a 'tight ship' remaining efficient, skilful and on top of the situation at all times. In other words, success in the licensed trade, like any other, requires a totally professional approach.

Happily that professionalism includes enjoying yourself with a wide variety of interesting and genial people, in exchange for merely putting yourself out a bit. The publican's lot, unlike the policeman's, can be a happy one.

Basic policy

Let us start right away by bringing that professionalism to bear. In business there is no room for a haphazard approach. A casual attitude and sloppy or non-existent planning inevitably lead to inefficiency which in turn causes frustration and aggravation all round. Everything must be done in a logical and structured way, but neither logic nor structure will stand up unless built on a secure foundation.

Even at this early stage you are undoubtedly making plans, visualising the sort of pub you want, developing ideas about how you will run it. You will soon have to make major decisions about which part of the country you want to live and work in, which particular pub to choose, how you will decorate and furnish it, which products to stock, and many more.

It is therefore essential to set out, right now, what is to be the underlying philosophy, the basic policy, that will form the foundation of your business. Once you have done this, and it is firmly fixed in your mind, then all the decisions you have to make now and in the future will become that much easier.

What is that policy to be? The basic principles have already been outlined in this chapter. We have seen that you, as a publican, will be selling a certain atmosphere or ambience, a feeling of comfort and well-being. This is achieved fundamentally by your positive and genial attitude, which not only has an obvious and direct effect on your customers, but is also reflected in everything about the pub—the decor and furnishings for example—which in turn produce that atmosphere.

The fundamental reason for having any business is, of course, to make money. To achieve that aim in a pub means keeping in the forefront of your mind the need to make all present and future customers feel psychologically and physically comfortable and at home so that they will want to stay, spending money, and also want to come back again and again.

Thus, as each problem arises, the solution will be the one that will most successfully fulfil the requirements of your policy.

The secret of success

Here, then, you have the secret of your success: total professionalism in the application of your basic business policy. It is as simple, and at the same time as difficult, as that. If your enterprise starts to falter, if things do not work out as you expected, then go back to that basic recipe. You can be sure that you have, in some way, not followed its principles. Now let us start applying them.

Chapter 2
Finding Your Pub

There are three avenues to becoming a publican: you can work for a brewery as a pub manager, you can take on the tenancy of a tied house which you rent from a brewery, or you can purchase your own free house outright.

Entry into the trade

Your choice may to some extent be governed by inclination. As a *manager* you do not have to bear the risks attached to ownership, but you are almost completely under brewery control. For a *tenant* the risk factor is kept within bounds, but there is still a degree of brewery control. As the *owner* of a free house you take on all the risk, but enjoy complete freedom and reap all the rewards.

The main consideration, however, is usually availability of capital. A manager does not need any, except in some cases a small amount as a fidelity bond. A tenant has to purchase the fixtures, fittings and stock, may feel the need to spend some money on refurbishment, will need some working capital, and will probably have to make a refundable security deposit with the brewery as a safeguard against non-payment of the trading account.

To purchase a free house requires a considerable sum, from about £70,000 to £150,000 for most pubs, rising to £500,000 and more for some. These are freehold prices, of course. Leasehold properties can be bought for considerably less, but do have their drawbacks, as we shall see later. The fact that you do not have this much money is not necessarily an insuperable obstacle as there are ways of raising the difference. However, against this must be balanced the

20

cost of servicing the loan. Let us look at the three methods in more detail.

Management

A manager is a salaried employee of the brewer. He will apply for a position in the same way as for any other job. Very often his wife is expected to take a share of the duties and responsibilities for which she will receive a small retainer. Couples with families are not normally considered.

There will be a training period during which he will not only learn the art of running a pub, but also the company's system of book-keeping and stock control. This is generally followed by a period as a relief manager, looking after establishments while people are on leave.

As a manager he will be paid a salary which is not usually particularly high, but his accommodation, rates and fuel bills are all paid for him. In addition most brewers run incentive schemes. Furthermore, the catering side of the operation is usually left to the manager. He will probably have to pay a franchise fee and all the expenses, including the wages of the catering staff. The profits, however, are all his, and as brewery-managed houses are often large, successful enterprises, these can be considerable.

At the end of the day, a good manager in a good pub may well be better off than a brewery tenant, or even a free house proprietor. At the same time he is answerable to the brewer for the efficient running of a large enterprise. His responsibilities are considerable, and he must continually earn the confidence of his employer.

Tenancy

The tenant of a tied house rents the premises from the brewer, who is usually responsible for the upkeep, decoration and insurance of the building, except for the private quarters in some cases. In view of the very considerable costs of repairs to what are so often buildings of great age, this can be a powerful argument for the consideration of a tenancy, as opposed to the purchase of a free house.

Running Your Own Pub

By the terms of his contract the tenant has to buy all his supplies of beer, usually the wines, spirits and soft drinks, and sometimes cigarettes, tobacco, crisps and nuts, from the brewer. The prices he has to pay for wines, spirits and soft drinks are usually considerably higher than he would have to pay elsewhere. It can be annoying to find items on sale in the local supermarket at a lower price than you have to pay the brewer. In addition, most brewers take a proportion of the profits from fruit machines, video games and pool tables which must be leased from operators stipulated by them.

You are, therefore, unable to stock the products of other brewers, with a few exceptions such as Guinness. This can be irritating, especially when someone walks out of the door because you do not have his favourite brew. However, as most brewers nowadays have very similar ranges and there is usually an acceptable alternative, this is not an insurmountable problem.

The major advantages of a tied house, then, are the relatively low initial capital outlay and the savings on repairs and renovations to the building. Against this must be set the lower potential profit margin in view of the higher price you are charged for some supplies, the rental, and the loss of a proportion of the profits on amusement machines.

Rents are often calculated on the basis of the number of barrels of beer sold per year. Therefore when, as a result of your hard work and business acumen, trade increases, the gilt tends to be taken off the gingerbread by a rent rise.

It must also be remembered that however successful you have been, however much you have managed to increase the turnover of the house, when you wish to leave you will have only the fixtures and fittings to sell. If they should be the ones you bought when taking over, they will in fact have depreciated in value. In other words, you will gain nothing from the goodwill you have created, and your initial capital outlay may well have decreased in value.

This could be a very serious matter for someone at retiring age, especially during a period of high

Finding Your Pub

inflation, unless a quite considerable proportion of income has been put away for the provision of a home and pension.

But whatever the drawbacks, it is true to say that the tied-house system does offer those of limited means a unique opportunity of going into business on their own account in a trade where the opportunities are almost unlimited.

Ownership
The purchase of a free house outright is, if you have the resources, usually the most desirable method. You have no rent to pay, you can choose which products to stock, and you can shop around for the most competitive prices. Unlike the tied house, the property itself usually appreciates in value, the more so if, by means of greater turnover, the goodwill element has increased.

Against this must be set the high cost of the up-keep of the building and, if a loan has been necessary to raise the initial purchase price, the high cost of servicing it. In the event of the enterprise failing the potential loss can be considerable. And it must be remembered that businesses *can* fail, often through no fault of their owners. A period of recession can have grave consequences, while many pubs have suffered from the building of a bypass, or the unexpected closure of a factory which supplied a large proportion of their clientele.

Leasehold
There are many leasehold pubs in existence, but their only real attraction is a somewhat lower price than a similar freehold property. Against this must be set the following considerations: finance is very much harder to obtain; there is a high rental to pay which is usually reviewed (ie, increased) every few years; you are responsible for all repairs and renovations; your initial investment will depreciate dramatically in value as the term of the lease shortens; a short-term lease is almost impossible to sell and renewal is by no means guaranteed. Furthermore, leasehold pubs are often owned by breweries who require a tie, in which

23

case a tied-house tenancy may be preferable. In any event, be very sure about what you are taking on, and seek the advice of your accountant and solicitor. Remember that your profits will have to cover, not only the rental and any interest charges, but also a heavy depreciation.

Professional advice

Which way into the trade you choose depends mainly on the availability of capital. Other factors are the degree of independence you desire, the degree of risk you are prepared to consider, the income you require, and how you envisage your situation when you finally leave the trade.

This can be a difficult decision. Do not make it unaided. There are plenty of people, part of whose job is to give advice. Do not hesitate to use them.

Your bank manager is a mine of information, and should perhaps be your first contact. He knows your financial situation, can tell you how much finance you can expect to raise, and what it will cost. He should have a fair idea of the returns to be expected in the trade. He will not hesitate to be blunt if he feels that you are making a wrong move.

Be professional about this. When it comes to raising finance one of the most important factors that will be taken into account is your apparent business ability. You will not make a great impression if the relevant facts are not at your fingertips. Write down an outline of the sort of pub you are considering. Break down the estimated total cost into its various components as set out on page 34. List all your capital resources including any you do not intend to realise for this venture.

Obviously, the manager cannot give definite answers until you have a definite proposition, but with this information he can give you a general guide so that you at least have an idea of the price range you can consider.

Do not hesitate to see another bank manager, especially if you feel that your present one is not quite up to the mark. And if you are going for a pub outside your present locality, consult more than one in the new area. They are invaluable for local information, and may even know something of the history of the business you are considering.

The same applies to accountants, although they may, quite reasonably, charge a nominal sum for their advice. This is money well spent. They can give a remarkably clear picture of costs and expected profits, but do not let them unwittingly bamboozle you with their jargon. Make sure you understand what they mean. Do not be afraid to ask for clarification.

Solicitors can be most helpful. They also usually have a sound knowledge of local affairs and can sometimes assist in matters of finance.

Fellow publicans, brewers, licensed brokers (the estate agents of the trade), finance houses, the trade press, the local Licensed Victuallers Association, any businessman, are all good sources of information. People like airing their knowledge. Give them the opportunity.

Organising the search

You must, first of all, have a fair idea of the sort of pub you are looking for. It must primarily be one that fits your personality, one in which you will feel comfortable and at home. You can hardly be a good host if you feel out of place yourself. Take a careful look at your present favourite drinking places and work out what it is that you like about them. It is likely that these aspects will influence the choice of your own place.

You will need to decide whether you want a town-centre pub, one on a housing estate, in a village, or way out in the country; whether it is to be a small, easily managed place, or with potential to expand. Do you need extra space for a restaurant or function room? How much private accommodation do you require? Are you envisaging a beer garden? Write down the answers to these questions, and add any other requirements you may have in mind. It is unlikely that you will find a pub to fit exactly, but it helps to prevent yourself getting carried away by a

25

place that looks irresistible, but is in fact totally unsuitable for you.

You must also decide in which part of the country you would like to live and work. It is not wise to narrow the area too drastically as this will considerably reduce the number of suitable pubs likely to become available. Keep in mind, however, that you may have to adjust to a different way of life, new customs, and an unfamiliar accent in a district new to you.

Factors to be taken into account in considering particular areas are the population density, the amount of unemployment, the general wage level and degree of prosperity, seasonal fluctuations, large numbers of retired people, threatened industries and so on. On a personal level you may have to think of schooling for the children, facilities for your own recreation and distance from relatives and elderly parents.

Now order the *Morning Advertiser*, the trade's daily paper, from your newsagent. You may see properties of interest advertised but, as there will be many which do not appear, write to all the brokers and agents in any case. Keep watching the columns of the *Morning Advertiser* and of any other trade publications you can get hold of. The landlord of your local may be helpful here. Sometimes properties are advertised privately, and every so often a broker will pop up who you have not written to before.

If you are seeking a tenancy write also to all the breweries, as only some brokers handle tied houses. Some breweries will pass you on to a broker, but many handle their own brokerage.

Details of pubs will start to flood in. Go through them carefully, but be absolutely ruthless in rejecting those which do not really fit the bill, however attractive they look. You could spend a lifetime, and a fortune, rushing around the countryside looking at unsuitable places which could have been easily weeded out by a careful study of the details at home.

Try to organise trips in such a way as to cover several pubs in the same general area at the same time. Check the map for their position and plan a route before you set off. I have always found it best to pop in for a quiet drink before making any definite arrangements to view. On the majority of occasions this is all that is required to reject the place, and your time, and that of the landlord is thereby saved.

But please do be discreet. Many landlords do not like their regulars and staff to become unsettled by finding out in advance about their plans to leave. Just have a quiet, unobtrusive look around, and avoid, at this stage, intensive questioning of the locals. If you like the look of it, and it fulfils a good proportion of your requirements, then is the time to make an appointment to view.

What to look for

Much of what you need to know, if only to reject the place, will be contained in the details sent to you. Whether it is in the right part of the country and the right sort of locality; the number of bedrooms; the overall size of the property; has it a car park or a garden?; and whatever other factors are of interest to you.

Car parking facilities are particularly important. You are unlikely to have sufficient customers within walking distance, and nothing puts off a motorist more quickly than a frustrating search for a vacant space. Street parking is rarely sufficient. Be sure there are enough facilities and, if you are considering making more space, check with the local planning office to see if there are likely to be any snags.

As you approach a pub have a look at the surrounding district. Note whether it is basically industrial or residential, and whether it looks run-down or prosperous. Check whether there are many other pubs around, and whether this pub is in a backwater or in a busy area with plenty of passing trade. Is it easy to find and to get to?

Your first glimpse of the outside will probably have an immediate effect on your opinion. As with buying houses, emotion often has a major influence. This is not wholly bad. After all, you will have to live and work in the place for some years, and it will do you or your business little good if it depresses you.

Running Your Own Pub

However, do not let a charming looking building blind you to its drawbacks, or let an unprepossessing one put you off until you have given some consideration as to how you could improve its appearance (see Chapter 4). At the same time bear in mind that what puts you off may well put customers off as well.

Have a quick look at the structural and decorative condition, especially if you are buying. Are there any cracks? Does the roof dip in places? Be suspicious of roofs which have been treated with coats of tar or bitumen as this is usually a stop-gap measure on one which really needs replacing. Check the window frames and sills for obvious signs of rot.

According to the time of day, notice the number of cars outside and the number of customers inside. Is there plenty of parking space and is there a garden? If it is obvious that the inside is badly arranged, check whether major alterations would be required to sort it out. Is it big enough to accommodate your plans for expansion, or indeed simply to fit in the number of customers you are expecting to win?

Do not be put off right away if trade is obviously bad and the place is dirty or dreary. Consider the reasons for it, and whether you feel you can do something about it. In many cases the best pub to take over is a run-down one. At least you should be able to do better, and it is easier to stamp your personality on a previously neglected establishment than on one strongly influenced by the character of a successful landlord.

If it passes this initial test then arrange to view. Do try to fit in with the landlord's convenience. You will get far more cooperation from him when he is not pressed or harassed. How much you find out about the business will largely depend on that cooperation.

It is a good idea to take notes when you view, and draw a rough sketch plan. Important details are very easily forgotten after you have traipsed around half a dozen pubs. You will need to note whether the private quarters are big enough for your needs; whether there is sufficient room at present, or potentially, for the trade you expect to do; whether the bar is long enough to cater for a reasonable number at one time,

28

Finding Your Pub

and if there is enough room behind it for several people to work easily and efficiently; whether the kitchen is large enough for your projected needs. Is there a cellar and plenty of suitable storage space for bottled beers, wines, spirits, soft-drinks, catering dry goods, freezers and refrigerators, machinery and equipment?

Note the things that you may have to spend money on—toilets, electric wiring, catering equipment, decorations, furniture and carpets. Are the heating arrangements sufficient and reasonably cost effective?

You may at this stage still be sufficiently interested to ask to see the accounts. Many landlords can be quite cagey at this point, especially if it is a tenancy. Do not worry too much. Get his accountant's address and leave it to your accountant to request copies. In any case, it is far better to go over them with the experts who will be able to tell you exactly what sort of story they tell.

After leaving take a closer look at the surrounding district. Call in nearby pubs and gauge the competition. Look around at the potential sources of custom such as housing estates, factories, sports facilities, colleges, industrial estates, tourist attractions and areas of large population.

Talk to people about the area and about the pub. What sort of reputation has it got? Is it declining? Was it once the 'in place' to go? Is it known as the fighting pub, the posh place, popular with young people or a haunt of drunks and down-and-outs? Ask if the area is prosperous, or if local industries are declining. Find out about the average wage levels and how many are out of work.

Estate agents will have population figures, and will know of plans for new residential or industrial development. Similar information can be gleaned from the local planning office, who will also tell you if a bypass is about to be built, or a motorway to be blasted through the pub's beer garden. Furthermore, they may be able to advise whether there is likely to be any difficulty over plans you may have to extend the buildings or car park. And while you are at it ask local policy regarding pub signs, as it can make quite a difference to your attempts to bring people in (see Chapter 4).

If appropriate, the local tourist office is worth a visit to get some idea of the scale of tourism in the area, and to discover any attractions within reach of the pub.

If you do not have time to do this on the same day, go back again, or better still stay for a night or two in the area. You cannot get too much information, and the more you have the easier it will be to decide if this is the place for you.

Potential profitability

Your accountant, once he has seen the accounts, will be able to tell you whether the business is at present sufficiently profitable to provide a reasonable income. He will also be able to indicate whether trade is on the increase or in decline.

Do not imagine, however, that things will remain the same when you take over. As already pointed out, the landlord *is* the pub. Simply because you are a different person the pub will be different. Consequently, some customers will leave along with the previous landlord, and hopefully some new ones will take their place. You cannot, therefore, afford to be complacent, however healthy the accounts. You must presume the necessity to expand, although your ambitions might drive you in that direction anyway.

What you now have to decide is whether the area contains the potential for an increase in trade, and whether the pub has the basic features which can be developed to attract it. In your reconnaissance you should have gained a fair idea of where the customers might come from. You should also have gathered whether they are being catered for elsewhere. For example, a large factory may have its own canteen and bar, and cannot, therefore, be relied upon to provide a good lunch-time trade. The pub down the road with its disco, amusement machines and games may have already captured the young market. The tourists will almost certainly go to the pub nearest to the attraction they have come to see.

The most important consideration is simply the sheer number of people living within reach. The traditional question is, 'How many chimneys are around?' The immediate locality will produce your bread-and-butter trade. If there is a big enough population and not obviously too many pubs catering for them, *and* you bring the basic policy outlined in Chapter 1 to bear, then you should be able to attract your share.

Once again, write all these points down. Make a list of pros and cons, and do not hesitate to reject the place if it does not stand up to the test. Before going ahead, be confident that it can produce a good living, remembering that before long you will probably have to convince others. Do not brush aside niggling doubts. Face them, analyse them, and be sure of their importance or otherwise.

Raising the finance

Finance is an invaluable business tool, a useful way to get a project off the ground. The lender is also a businessman who, in a way, becomes your partner, inasmuch as he has invested in your enterprise, is sharing the risks, and expecting to make a profit.

Finance is useless to you unless it achieves its object, which is to create a viable business. In other words, if that finance costs more than the business can safely bear, just as if you draw out vast sums for your own riotous living, then it will eventually destroy that which it was designed to create.

So do not set your heart on a particular pub and go all out, bull-headed, to get it, regardless of cost, or how much you have to borrow. Cool judgement is required, based on the hard facts of the situation. You must be utterly convinced that it is a sound business proposition that will comfortably withstand the servicing of any loans required. You will be going to your bank manager, or a finance house, not as though he was some sort of adversary from whom to extract the maximum amount by fair means or foul, but as an experienced businessman who wants to do business with you, and wants your enterprise to succeed so that he may share in the profits. His experience and expertise are considerable. If he knows all the facts of the case he can determine whether it is a viable proposition. But his assessment is not just to help him decide whether to risk his money, it is also to help *you* discover whether you have a fair chance of success. If he says 'no', take his decision seriously. He knows what he is talking about, and your plan should be very carefully reconsidered, if not dropped entirely.

His funds can make him an invaluable partner: you have to convince him that your proposition, and your abilities and business acumen, are sufficiently sound for him to take the risk.

Presenting your case

You therefore have to present a case, remembering that it must satisfy *you* just as much as anyone else. In other words, what follows is the method by which, if you do the job properly and are completely honest, you can see for yourself whether your projected enterprise has a reasonable chance of success.

Write down, or type if you can, the following information in a clear and logical manner. Make the whole presentation neat, clear, tidy and *businesslike*.

About yourself

Whoever finances you will want to know what sort of person you are, all the more so because he knows that pubs rely largely on the personality of the landlord, as well as his business acumen and ability to work hard. So when you see him, remember that he will be looking at you as a potential publican, and will expect to find an outgoing, genial personality with enthusiasm, professionalism, and a confidence in his ability to succeed.

What experience do you have that is in any way relevant? For example, you may have worked behind the bar in your local; your present job may involve dealing with the public, handling cash, keeping the books, supervising staff or selling; perhaps you are an excellent cook; you may have experience running social events, a sports team or a club. Think hard: there is almost certain to be some aspect of your

Finding Your Pub

experience that will stand you in good stead in the pub trade.

Briefly jot these down with your age, state of health, and your own assessment of your abilities, not forgetting those qualities mentioned in the Introduction. Make a note also of the factors influencing your decision to give up your present occupation, and your reasons for wanting to take a pub. Let your enthusiasm be obvious.

Now list all your financial resources, whether or not you intend to use them for this venture. Include cash, savings, property and life insurances, also all your liabilities such as outstanding mortgages, loans, overdrafts and hire purchase commitments.

The pub
Briefly describe the pub using photographs and the broker's details if available. Note the accommodation, private as well as business, and how it is at present being used. Mention the structural and decorative condition, the car parking arrangements, the toilet facilities. Is it busy or run down? What sort of clientele is using it at present? Describe its situation, pointing out nearby population centres, industrial and business areas, sporting and tourist facilities, main roads and shopping centres. Detail the competition, including licensed clubs and bars, and explain why you think they pose no threat, or how you expect to improve on them.

The business
You will need the last three years' audited accounts. Let your accountant see them first, and get his comments on the picture they reveal.

Your plans
In what way do you expect to improve trade? By the introduction of catering, entertainment, a beer garden, a children's room, darts teams, a restaurant? How are you going to carry it out? You may feel that the basis for a healthy business is already there, and that what is required is your personality plus a good clean-up, redecoration, and the creation

33

Running Your Own Pub

of a warm, welcoming atmosphere.

Describe the sort of clientele you expect to attract, and where they will come from. Outline your advertising scheme and your projected staffing arrangements. Be clear, convincing and enthusiastic.

How much?

Now list your immediate capital requirements, such as:

- Purchase price (free house)
- Ingoings (tied house)
  - Inventory
  - Brewer's security deposit
  - Broker's fees
- Legal fees
- Removal expenses
- Licence fees
- Stock purchases
- Insurances
- Working capital
- Repairs
- Decorations
- Furniture
- Structural alterations
- Bar equipment
- Catering equipment
- Vehicle purchase

Total them up, and note how much you are going to have to borrow.

Cash flow projection

Now you have to show whether the business is capable of servicing the loan; that is, will there be sufficient funds at the end of the day to make the repayments? This is done by drawing up a cash flow projection for the next 12 months. You estimate what your income is going to be in each month, deduct your expenses, and you are then left with a cash figure out of which you will have to find the money for the loan repayment.

There is a typical example on pages 36-7. It is based on the accounts of the outgoing proprietor, and

34

Finding Your Pub

of necessity involves several assumptions such as:

Sales income and expenditure are all inclusive of VAT where appropriate.

Seasonal pattern of takings is built into the sales income.

Purchases are paid in the month they are received.

Liquor purchases are based on a gross margin of 35 per cent.

Food purchases are based on a gross margin of 65 per cent.

VAT payments are calculated on the basis of projected takings.

Opening balance reflects the net position after all existing assets are purchased and liabilities settled.

Stock levels remain constant throughout the year.

Wages reflect seasonal employment of casual staff.

These assumptions will have to be noted for the bank manager's information so that he understands what is going on.

Most of the figures are, of course, estimates, based on the previous figures, but reflecting what you reasonably expect to happen over the next 12 months. Thus, you may feel that you can reasonably expect to improve the income from sales by, say, 5 to 10 per cent, but allowance has to be made for seasonal fluctuation. You perhaps consider that you can manage with fewer staff, but are expecting beer prices to rise shortly by around 7 per cent, and estimate that the additional catering equipment you intend to purchase will push up your fuel bills by something like 10 per cent. All these points will be reflected in the difference between the figures in your projection, and the actual ones in the existing accounts, and will have to be explained to the bank manager. Remember that this is only showing the cash situation, and is not a profit and loss account.

You will notice in the example that the quieter winter months show an actual cash deficit, although by the end of the year there is a healthy surplus. This

35

Cash flow projection, subject to certain underlying assumptions (see page 35)

	Oct	Nov	Dec	Jan	Feb	Mar	Apr	May	June	July	Aug	Sept	Total
	£	£	£	£	£	£	£	£	£	£	£	£	£
INCOME FROM SALES													
Liquor	3,500	2,700	3,000	2,400	2,500	3,400	3,700	3,800	3,900	5,100	5,400	3,800	43,200
Food	1,100	800	900	700	700	1,100	1,300	1,500	1,600	2,600	2,800	1,900	17,000
Total	4,600	3,500	3,900	3,100	3,200	4,500	5,000	5,300	5,500	7,700	8,200	5,700	60,200
EXPENDITURE													
Liquor purchases	2,275	1,755	1,950	1,560	1,625	2,210	2,405	2,470	2,535	3,315	3,510	2,470	28,080
Food purchases	385	280	315	245	245	385	455	525	560	910	980	665	5,950
Rates	250	—	—	—	—	—	250	—	—	—	—	—	500
Fuel	—	—	450	—	—	500	—	—	—	—	—	400	1,800
Telephone	—	60	—	—	60	—	—	60	—	—	60	—	240
Wages	160	160	170	120	120	140	150	160	180	200	200	180	1,940
Car expenses	80	80	80	80	80	80	80	80	80	80	80	80	960
Advertising	60	60	60	60	60	60	60	60	60	60	60	60	780

Repairs	50	50	50	50	50	50	50	50	50	50	600
Insurances	600										600
Sundries	50	50	50	50	50	50	50	50	50	50	600
Personal Drawings	200	200	200	200	200	200	200	200	200	200	2,400
VAT			920		815		1,300				3,035
Total	4,110	2,695	3,325	3,285	2,490	3,675	4,515	3,655	4,185	5,210	47,485

CASH FLOW

Net monthly cash flow (Total expenditure deducted from sales income)	490	805	575	−185	710	825	485	1,645	1,315	1,515	12,715
Add opening balance (ie the cash on hand at the start of each month)	1,000	790	895	770	−115	−105	20	−195	750	1,365	2,180
Deduct loan interest	700	700	700	700	700	700	700	700	700	700	8,400
Closing balance	790	895	770	−115	−105	20	−195	750	1,365	2,180	5,315

shows just how valuable such a projection can be for your own peace of mind. If you are expecting a shortfall, when it comes you are not caused unnecessary worry because you know that you can expect the situation to right itself in due course. Furthermore, you can see right away that in a few months' time you will be needing overdraft facilities. It is far better, and much more businesslike, to make the arrangements now, after having shown the bank manager why they will be needed, than to approach him in a panic at the time. He may well jump to the conclusion that things are going badly wrong, and not feel inclined to throw good money after bad.

But overall, what the example of a cash flow projection shows in this particular case is that, as long as things go according to plan, the loan repayments can be met with the help of a small overdraft for a four-month period. What is more, it appears that there will be a sufficient cash surplus by the end of the year to take care of any unforeseen hiccups and provide a good basis for the following year.

Your bank manager may be grateful to receive these figures a few days before any formal meeting. This gives him a chance to review the proposition and formulate questions.

Shop around

As I said before, if your first approach is turned down, take note of the reasons and look again at your proposition with a critical eye. Do not be afraid to throw it out, however attractive it may seem to you. There will be other opportunities and you will not thank yourself in a few months' time if you end up with an insupportable millstone round your neck.

But if you are still utterly convinced of its soundness there is no need to admit defeat. Try another bank manager or approach finance houses. Your broker may well be able to recommend somebody. A few building societies will consider mortgages, and solicitors occasionally have access to suitable funds.

Brewers are normally very willing to help in return for an agreement to sell a minimum quantity of their products. This quantity varies according to the amount borrowed. As a result of this partial tie they are willing to charge very low interest rates, but are not usually able to lend very large amounts. Try several breweries as their terms vary widely.

I would not recommend approaching friends or relations. Business and friendship rarely mix, and if things do go wrong it is not very pleasant to lose the money of your nearest and dearest.

I cannot stress too heavily the need for caution when piling debts on your plate. Interest charges, so lightly taken on in the first flush of enthusiasm, can quickly turn into a crippling responsibility.

Make sure that you know exactly what rate you are being charged, and what your repayments are going to be. Satisfy yourself, with the help of your cash flow projection, that they are well within your budget. Let your accountant see what you are letting yourself in for and *take his advice*.

Negotiating a tenancy

Good tenancies are generally highly sought after, and all of them have a large number of applicants. If you are to obtain the one you want then you have to convince the brewers that you are by far the best person for the pub in question. They are business-men, interested primarily in the maximum sales of their products. Therefore, they are looking for some-one who is also first and foremost a businessman, who understands the way in which those products are marketed, and who has the acumen, ability and enthusiasm to develop their mutual interests suc-cessfully.

Brewers seek their tenants in different ways. Some do it directly as a result of your direct application to them. Others do it through brokers who will weed out the applicants down to just two or three who they think are the most suitable, and then pass them on for final selection.

In either case you will be interviewed, perhaps two or three times. All your efforts must therefore be directed towards impressing the interviewer with your abilities. Professionalism comes to the fore again, and if you are to have a hope of success you will have to spare no pains to present a convincing case.

Your personality will be under close scrutiny. This does not call for a hearty, backslapping approach, but a polite, cheerful, enthusiastic and businesslike attitude, tinged with a modest confidence in your ability to do the job. Keep in mind what you are being interviewed for, and stick to what the interviewer *wants* to hear. There is no point in telling him about what you can't or don't like doing. He will not be interested in your troubles, or in tedious explanations of your past exploits. Emphasise those points about yourself which are relevant to the trade you hope to enter, and demonstrate a positive attitude to life and work. He will want to know about any experience you have which will in any way stand you in good stead, such as bar work, dealing with the public, handling cash and accounts, selling, buying, organising social events, catering and so on. He will expect to see a well-dressed, genial and healthy person.

Your financial situation will be checked, so come armed with all the figures, and show, not only that you have adequate resources, but that you have gone about calculating your needs and raising finance in a businesslike way.

Most of all, you will have to demonstrate to your interviewer that you have thoroughly investigated the pub in question, that you are yourself convinced that you can create a viable and successful enterprise with it, and that you are the best person to do it. Therefore, all the information you have gathered to satisfy yourself and your bank manager can now be brought forward to press your case to the brewer. Tell him how you see the business at the moment, what sort of trade it is attracting, and where from, avoiding any sort of criticism of the present tenant. Explain your basic business policy and how you would apply it in this particular case. Point out what can be done to develop the right atmosphere, and to attract the elements of the public which are not at present being catered for. Detail the competition and what you intend to do about it. Show him population figures, maps of the area, plans of your proposals regarding better use of the pub's facilities. Discuss your advertising and publicity schemes and your ideas about the development of the 'package' you intend to present to the public. Seek his opinions and ideas. Let him see your accountant's comments and your cash flow projection. Make him understand that you have a firm grasp of the problems, sound answers to them, and a factually based optimism about the future.

Have all this down in writing, and if the opportunity presents itself, send a copy to him a few days before the interview so that he has plenty of time to digest and be impressed by it. His feelings about you will be greatly enhanced before the meeting even begins.

Such professionalism should win the day, but if you are unlucky do not let that depress you. Move on to the next opportunity, and approach that with the same enthusiasm and determination until you succeed.

Purchasing a free house

Once you have made the decision to buy it is good sense to go back for another look. You will be surprised how much you missed the first time. Make sure you know the exact boundaries, who is responsible for which walls and fences, whether there are any rights of way or easements, and that there are no ties or agreements which you will inherit.

The negotiations can become very impersonal, sometimes complicated, often frustrating. It is therefore important on this visit to establish good relations with the outgoing landlord, and to ensure that you are in full agreement about the price and precisely what you are buying. In the days ahead a quick telephone call to him can often clear up problems and misunderstandings which tend to get blown up out of all proportion by legal language, and which can cause quite extraordinary delays in the normal channels.

It will save interminable and expensive solicitors' correspondence if at this point you exchange solicitors' names and addresses, obtain the vendor's full name, and give him yours and your address. Also find out the name and address of the local authority, the address of the clerk to the licensing justices, and the days of the week on which the justices sit.

Advise your solicitor of your intended purchase and pass on all the above information. He will also need to know the purchase price and details of any loans you have contracted. Make sure he keeps you informed of developments, and do not hesitate to press him if too much time seems to be passing. Let the agent or broker earn his money if any chasing up needs to be done. Keep in touch with the vendor to ensure that all goes according to plan.

At the same time, go back to the bank or finance company with all the information you have gathered, including copies of the present landlord's accounts and your accountant's comments. Almost invariably they will want a survey of the premises, but it is unlikely that you will have a sight of the report. It is wise therefore to have a survey carried out yourself.

Change-over day

While awaiting completion, do as much as possible to prepare for change-over day and the start of business. Initiate your bank accounts and register the business name if necessary. Your bank will furnish the appropriate form. Set up an office organisation, filing system and the stocktaking record cards. Purchase the account, signing-in and wages books. Register for VAT (with HM Customs and Excise), and apply to the Inland Revenue for the forms and tables for PAYE and National Insurance contributions. Test, compare and select the products of potential suppliers. Make up menus and order provisions. Liaise with the outgoing landlord to ascertain what liquor stocks you will need to order for delivery on the first day. It is customary to save work and stocktaker's fees by running stocks down. Consequently, you will require somewhat more than the normal weekly order, especially as your first few days will probably be a little busier than usual while the locals come to give you the once-over. The brewers usually

42

Finding Your Pub

have fixed delivery days, but traditionally make exception for change-over day.

Prepare any notices and blackboards you require, and have appropriate signs made. Arrange for the reading of gas and electricity meters, and the transfer of the accounts into your name. Order heating oil and solid fuel if necessary. Arrange for the transfer of the telephone. Organise the details of the move and of your first day in order to minimise the stress of those initial hectic hours.

By opening time in the morning you must be ready for business, and as the regulars will take this opportunity to 'give the new bloke a look-over' you should ideally be at your best, despite the many distractions and tensions of the day.

It is convenient if you can arrange for the outgoing landlord to move his furniture out on the previous day. Organise things so that you do not have to spend time humping furniture yourself. Label everything so that the removal men know where they are to go with minimum supervision. As far as the private quarters go, the only item which it is essential to concern yourself with is the bed, to ensure a much needed night's sleep. Everything else will get sorted out gradually in the days ahead.

Your first duty will be to attend the local magistrates' court with the outgoing licensee and your solicitor, who will already have notified the court and advised the police. They will have checked whether you have a criminal record and may have made enquiries in your home district about your character and reputation. They will be asked whether they have any objection to you holding a liquor licence. The magistrates may well ask you a few questions about yourself and will probably have a few words of advice and warning. If all is well a protection order will be granted—a sort of temporary licence which will last until the next full transfer session when you will have to go back to court for the full licence.

Back at the pub the stocktaker will have arrived. He will usually be arranged for by the broker, and will have to be paid on the spot. His duties are to list and value all the stocks of liquor, glassware and fuel

43

Running Your Own Pub

which you will then pay for.

Once this has been done you are ready for business and must put a float in the till. You will need plenty of coins and notes of every denomination up to £5 from the bank well beforehand. I would suggest a minimum of 25 one-penny pieces, 50 pence in two-pence pieces, £1 in five-pence pieces, £5 of 10-pence pieces, £10 of 50-pence pieces, 20 £1 coins and one £5 note. You should have plenty more to hand. Running out of change is embarrassing, annoying to the customer, and time-wasting. It does not lend credibility to your professionalism!

As you will still have plenty of distractions, and as this will be your first time behind an unfamiliar bar, it is a good idea to have someone else to serve at this session. You will then be able to give your full attention to the business in hand, and to public relations work.

The inventory, or list of furniture and fittings, will be verified by your brokers. Deliveries will start to arrive and must be checked in. To ensure the continued cooperation of the brewers' draymen in the months ahead it is a good idea to offer them a drink. Representatives of all sorts will descend upon you at the same time, not usually expecting to talk business, but as a gesture of goodwill. Certainly this is not a day to allow yourself to be pressurised into buying. Tell them to return in a few weeks, once the dust has settled.

They and many others will be pressing you to accept a drink. It is wise not to offend the regulars by refusing, but do go steady. It will be a long day and you need to keep your wits about you if you are to make the right impression. For that reason, and for the sake of good customer relations, do not in any circumstances indulge in the stronger more expensive drinks.

Although you will be busy it is essential to bring your basic business policy into operation right away. On this day in particular you will be under scrutiny by the locals. An open, friendly and positive attitude should ensure that they will continue to use the pub. Word will quickly spread.

Finding Your Pub

Especially in a small community, it is often customary for a new landlord to buy everyone a drink on the first day. It is quite an effective public relations exercise and, if looked at in that light, not particularly expensive. Remember also that free drinks do encourage a festive mood which in turn generates increased consumption. In other words, your initial investment may well bring increased sales as well as popularity.

Chapter 3
The Customer

In Chapter 1 we discussed why people go to a pub and from the answer developed a basic business policy of cultivating a positive, responsive and genial frame of mind concentrated on the well-being of the customer. This attitude is entirely consistent with the overall business objective of making money, because it directs your efforts towards encouraging your customers to spend freely while they are in your establishment and to creating a desire within them to return, again and again. For a pub, probably more than most other enterprises, depends on repeat business. What someone spends today pales into insignificance compared with the considerable sums they may lay out over the coming years. And so, even if they have only come to ask directions, or use the toilet, they are nevertheless potential spenders. You should ensure that they go away wanting to come back.

At one time I had a couple who visited my pub only twice a year. They spent the winter in southern England and the summer in the north. They made a point of calling in on their way back and forth. It hardly seemed worth encouraging such infrequent patrons, but I used to reflect that if I had enough of them throughout the year they would still fill the pub.

The customer's wants and needs

The customer does not consciously consider his total well-being. As far as he is concerned, he has simply come for a drink, and perhaps a meal. It is, of course, your responsibility to cater for those conscious desires, but more importantly, you have to try at the same time to satisfy the needs of which he is probably

46

scarcely aware. He needs to relax, and to do so fully he must feel 'at home'. That means that all the worries and stresses of the outside world should become remote. He should be aware that he is wanted and respected, that he is in a warm, safe, protected environment, surrounded by cheerful, unthreatening people who are concerned about his comfort and welfare. Alcohol helps tremendously, but it is also essential that for a while he feels cut off from the realities of everyday life.

First impressions
As he walks in the door he will take a quick look around. This is the moment he forms his first impression, and if he is a new customer it will have a lot to do with the actual appearance of the place. He notices, albeit more or less subconsciously, whether the room is warm and clean and if it has a cosy and welcoming feel about it. Much of this initial impression will be based on the individual's unique and personal experience, and his instincts about what constitutes a 'welcoming feel'. However, you can create an environment designed to induce these feelings in the majority of people, as will be demonstrated in Chapter 4.

Next, his attention will be directed towards the bar. What he will hope to find there is a friendly person, whose attitude implies that he is ready and willing to serve. Even if you are busy serving someone else, a cheerful greeting means that he has been noticed, that you acknowledge his importance to you as a customer, and that you will attend to his requirements as soon as possible.

Such a greeting has tremendous importance, for it sets the mood of the interchange that will take place between you for the rest of his stay. Once that initial contact has been made it is far less likely that he will decide he does not like the place, and far harder for him to turn around and walk out in any case.

Moreover, such a positive start to the relationship sets your own attitude towards him on the right plane. Your cheery, 'Good morning' affects your mood as well as his. It may be that after a heavy night you are feeling several degrees under, and your good humour seems reluctant to bubble to the surface in its accustomed manner. However, it is surprising how your apparent cheerfulness turns into the real thing after a few pleasant exchanges.

Carry this mood through. Be helpful in serving him. For example, many people will simply ask for a pint of bitter. It is your job to point out the choices available to him, and to check whether he prefers a straight glass or one with a handle. Indicate the various brands that you stock if he wants whisky, gin, or sherry. Do not wait for him to ask for ice, water, lemon, a cherry — offer them yourself. It is important to make sure that he knows what *is* available. A customer will often grudgingly go without his favourite drink rather than ask for it, simply because he cannot see it on the shelf.

The follow-up

Once these immediate needs have been taken care of, be discreetly attentive. Even while you are drawing the next customer's pint, glance around the bar and look out for all the little signs that show that someone is waiting for your attention. Very few people, thank goodness, rap impatiently on the counter when wanting service. Most are polite enough to wait patiently, but this puts the onus on the barman to notice that they require service.

In fact, it is not difficult to keep an eye on the state of the drinks of all the people at the bar, and to appear quietly soon after you notice a glass emptied and put down. It is often said that one of the highest attributes of a good barman, both from the landlord's and the customer's point of view, is 'a keen eye for an empty glass'. There have actually been studies made which have shown that, overall, the faster the service the greater the consumption, so it is not merely being polite to anticipate people's requirements and serve them quickly.

Customer relations

If there is a lull in serving pick out the chap who is

sitting at the bar alone, or the couple who appear to have run out of conversation. It is a safe bet that they would like to chat; they would go off to a private corner if they wanted to be left to themselves.

There are two simple secrets to the art of casual conversation: ask questions (of a general rather than too personal nature) and then *listen* to the answers. Try to curb your own desire to air your knowledge, or tell your own tale. It is a strange fact of human nature that you are more likely to be considered a hell of a good fellow if you listen to other people's opinions of themselves rather than if you try to point out your own undoubted virtues.

People remember and have good feelings about a pub where the landlord has passed the time of day with them. They will be back.

Complaints
Keep an eye out for the person who is obviously unhappy about something. Most people hate to complain and will sit staring at their cloudy beer, or playing with their cold steak and kidney pie, rather than make a fuss. Ask if anything is wrong and deal with it right away. If somebody does make a complaint respond helpfully in the knowledge that you have the power to do something about it: to put things right. Never take it as some sort of criticism or personal insult, or by your manner invite an aggressive response. Be pleasant and apologetic. Always replace the offending item, or refund the money immediately, however much the customer may protest that it is not necessary. He is thus disarmed, and the thought uppermost in his mind will not be the complaint but the efficient and helpful way you dealt with it.

A satisfied customer may well come back many times, in which case the loss of the price of a drink or a meal will be amply justified. A dissatisfied one will never return, and will make sure that many other people hear of his unfortunate experience.

I once had a regular customer who found a foreign body in his pickle. 'It doesn't worry me at all,' he said, 'but I thought I should tell you in case someone

Running Your Own Pub

else complained.' I apologised, and replaced the pickle. Because of the way he played it down I thought no more of it. The next day the Health Inspector turned up to investigate 'a serious complaint', and for weeks afterwards I heard how this chap was telling the story to everyone in the district. He vowed he would never set foot in the pub again because of the way I had handled his complaint!

On the other side of the coin I purchased a pint at one of my favourite pubs and did not discover that it was cloudy and undrinkable until I was in the beer garden. The barman saw me come back through the door with a full glass, instantly summed up the situation, and had apologised and drawn a fresh, clear pint before I had a chance to say anything. He thus not only saved me the embarrassment of complaining, but also forestalled any possibility of an unpleasant incident or of other customers realising that something was amiss.

Praise

It also does no harm to give people the chance to praise. Particularly with meals, the simple enquiry, 'Is everything all right?' not only shows your concern for their enjoyment, and that you value their opinion, but gives them the opportunity to put their favourable impressions into words. This might please you, but much more importantly it reinforces those impressions in their own minds. Furthermore, it gives them the chance to chat to you, and get to know you.

There is a sort of one-upmanship in claiming to 'know' the landlord of a pub. 'Oh yes, old Harry always does us proud when we go to the George.' They are trading on the fact that they are on intimate christian-name terms with the publican. It is a form of snobbery, but as they go around trying to impress their friends and acquaintances, just think of the advertising they are doing for you!

It is a good idea for you to learn and remember their names. We all like to be recognised by name. It gives us a distinct identity and a sense of self-importance. It contributes tremendously to our feeling of well-being.

And do not forget to say goodbye and thank-you as they leave. This is not only polite, but makes sure that their last impression is favourable, which reinforces the good feelings they have about you and your establishment. It shows that you consider them important enough to have noticed their departure, and that you have appreciated their custom.

None of this needs to be done in a servile way. An open, friendly and sincere attitude is all that is required. And there is no reason why it should not be genuinely sincere. After all, they have contributed to your livelihood, and have probably helped to make the session enjoyable for you.

Application of your basic policy
I hope you will have noticed that all this advice is based on the attitude dictated by your business policy: positive actions founded on a genuine desire to help or please people with the added attraction for yourself of increased business, now and in the future.

There is a sort of snowball effect. If people are relaxed and enjoying themselves, then each drink enhances the relaxation and enjoyment. As inhibitions disappear the money begins to flow more easily. Cocktails, brandies, liqueurs and expensive cigars are ordered. The world, and particularly your pub, comes to be seen as a hell of a nice place. Everybody, and particularly the landlord, is a hell of a nice fellow. You can be sure they will be back for more of the same.

And to a very large extent *you* have brought it all about.

Undesirable custom

There will inevitably be the occasional customer who most certainly will not make a session enjoyable for you or others. Unfortunately, where alcohol is being consumed there is bound to be the odd unwelcome incident.

My first piece of advice, which may sound strange, is to make sure that you do not actually *encourage* problems. For example, I took over a pub from a

Running Your Own Pub

landlord who proudly showed me the bloodstain on the concrete floor of the foyer where he had 'dealt with a small problem' the night before. He took great pride in his ability to handle himself when faced with trouble. Under the bar, spaced at intervals, were pieces of lead pipe, sawn-off billiard cues, and pickaxe handles. After I had enjoyed several weeks of entirely peaceful trading it dawned on me that he had, by his aggressive attitude, positively encouraged violence, just for the sheer enjoyment of demonstrating his skill at putting it down himself.

He could obviously look after himself, and the local young (and not so young) bucks saw him as a challenge, and came looking for some action. Once this focus of their aggression had gone, replaced by me, a boring, peaceful type only interested in polite and cheerful company, their interest rapidly waned.

One of the most effective, and least potentially dangerous ways of getting rid of someone that you suspect may be a nuisance, is simply to 'freeze' them out before they have the chance. If the landlord does not play his usual role of genial host, is not prepared to listen to their chatter, and makes it obvious by his attitude that they are not welcome, then what is there to stay for? They will soon move on to seek a more friendly establishment.

If trouble does arise, always maintain the sort of state of mind that in the motoring world is called 'defensive driving'. In other words do not be tempted to demonstrate your 'macho' qualities, or take an aggressive stance. Never become personally involved in any argument but take a position on the sideline. Try to defuse the situation in a calm but firm manner. Use your authority to demand good behaviour.

For as landlord, you do have authority, and not only that invested in you by law. People do generally respect your position as host, and therefore head of the house. Often trouble-makers will, like naughty children, obey your instructions if they are given firmly.

If things get out of hand do not attempt any physical interference, or allow your staff to do so. Quite

The Customer

apart from the risk of injury, you will probably further aggravate the situation and may well find that you end up facing a charge of assault. Warn that you will call the police, and if this has no effect do not hesitate to carry out your threat. Policemen are trained and are expert at handling such situations. Have no fear that they will feel that you should keep your own house in order. They have a duty to assist you, and prefer to keep the maintenance of law and order in their hands. Keep the local police telephone number in a prominent position by the phone. When you need it, you need it quickly.

Anyone who causes such problems should be immediately barred, and under no circumstances allowed to return. Such firmness will only gain the respect of other potential trouble-makers, and the peace of mind of your regular customers.

Chapter 4
The Pub and How to 'Sell' It

What you are selling is not so much drink or food as an atmosphere. That atmosphere is intimately linked with the landlord's personality, but the concrete expression of it is the pub—the building itself. Obviously, any feeling of homely welcome will largely stem from the physical appearance of the place, which will be an important part of the total picture which you try to build up in people's minds.

In a sense, therefore, you have to 'sell' the pub. You have to give people a reason to notice, and to want to come to, your establishment rather than any other. You need to create such a strong and lasting impression that your pub will be the first to spring to mind whenever they are thinking about going out for a drink or a meal.

Advertising

First, you have to let people know that the place exists. Whatever your pub may be offering, it is most important that as many people as possible know that you are there. If they are then occasionally reminded, sooner or later curiosity alone will bring them along. If, in addition, they hear that your beer, your food, your entertainment, or whatever, is particularly good, then it will more than likely be sooner than later.

Advertising in local newspapers and magazines is the method that first comes to mind. There is no doubt that this is very effective. People read their paper from cover to cover, and do notice the advertisements. Furthermore, they use it when wondering what to do or where to go on a night out.

The Pub and How to 'Sell' It

However, it is rather expensive to advertise on a regular basis, which is essential if it is to have any real effect. You must try to weigh the cost against the extra business you feel it brings in, plus the long-term publicity value of keeping your establishment in the public eye week after week.

The advertisements must be eye-catching. Some sort of logo is essential. The art department of the publication will probably help on this point.

Generally, confine your message to the aspects which you think are most likely to attract customers to your pub, cutting out any unnecessary 'waffle' which may cause the reader to quickly lose interest and turn the page. But dress up the important points with evocative adjectives. The pub might be 'cosy', or 'traditional', or 'fun'; the welcome 'warm'; the food 'home-cooked' and 'delicious'. Change the copy each week. This encourages people to read it; the same old story will just get passed over.

Be sure to include your address and telephone number, and brief directions to find the place if there is likely to be any difficulty.

Humour, reflecting the genial pub atmosphere, can be most effective. A little ditty, a joke, or an amusing, but short, tale about the place or its inmates can generate a lot of interest, and encourage people to make a point of looking each week to see your latest effort. One publican of my acquaintance advertised himself as 'the best looking landlord in town'. I thought he was an ugly brute myself, but he certainly packed them in!

Most local newspapers will do advertising features on a pub when a new landlord takes over, or perhaps when a new extension or facility has been added. This means that you get a one- or two-page spread for the price of your normal advertisement. Do not wait for the paper to approach you. As soon as you have a suitable excuse, get on to them.

Door-to-door leaflets
Door-to-door leaflets can be most effective. You can at least be sure that every household knows what you offer, and there is plenty of room for a large amount

55

of information. The cost is reasonable, and can be kept under control by covering areas just as and when the budget allows.

Posters and mailing
In Chapter 2 I suggested that you find out the potential sources of custom such as factories, colleges, and tourist attractions. It is a simple matter to ensure that these people know you are there. Ask if you can put posters up in factories, clubs, caravan parks, colleges, leisure complexes and tourist attractions. Write to business executives, solicitors, shops, offices, radio and TV stations, school staff rooms, anybody who might be interested in what your pub has to offer.

Publicity

The joy of publicity is that it can create most effective advertising while not costing you a penny. The aim is simply to keep your pub in the news. For example, local papers are always on the look out for a good story. Make sure you oblige them with plenty.

Get to know your local reporter. He will deem it a favour if you feed him information he can print. In quiet weeks he may well ring you for news. Even if it does not really concern your pub, you may well get a credit — 'The landlord of the George told this reporter . . .'

Before you take over the pub, contact him to suggest a few lines on the incoming landlord and his plans for the place. Extensions and renovations are newsworthy, as are happenings involving regulars such as a one hundredth birthday or '50 years' drinking in the same pub'.

Charity events you have organised, especially if they involve something unusual such as shaving half a head or a marathon pram race, are bound to get a mention. Eccentric or famous customers should always be reported, and make sure that if a visiting sports team drops in for a drink you get a mention in the match write-up.

Do not forget local radio. The news department will always be interested in local happenings. One pub I know finds every excuse to get a record request played for birthdays, anniversaries and local events. The pub name invariably gets into the dedication.

Gimmicks can be very useful, like the chap with the longest moustache in the world, a parrot or other unusual pet, or a friend of mine who cleaned his chimney with a blast from his 12-bore. One that has been successfully used by more than one landlord is to be extremely rude to the customers, but I am not sure that I would recommend it!

Organise events: get the local Morris Men to dance in your car park; challenge another pub to a football match or tug-of-war; have a yard-of-ale competition; give the local handicapped children a day out; raft races, car rallies, sponsored marathons, anything to keep you and your pub in the public eye.

Outside appearance

The outside appearance of your pub is the biggest, and should be the best advertisement you can ever have. Maybe thousands of people pass it every day. It should be good enough to ensure that they do not always go past. It is, if you like, the packaging around the goodies to be found inside.

Signs

Once again, first ensure that people know you are there; that it is a pub and not just another home or shop. This is the reason for the traditional swinging sign, which instantly identifies the building, but this is not enough. Such signs are not always in the best position to be seen, and do not really tell you much about the pub apart from its name.

Wherever practicable place signs 50 to 100 yards on either side of the building, giving motorists in particular time to digest the information and slow down. If they are permanent installations then you will need planning permission, but sandwich-board style signs, which can be taken in, are usually exempt. Check with the local planning authority.

57

If your situation is such that distant notices are out of the question, then the next best thing is a sandwich-board on the pavement immediately outside, with the message on both sides, or signs actually on the building at least, visible in both directions. Make sure that they are low enough, and the letters big enough, for passing motorists to read quickly and easily. Try them out yourself, both driving and walking: your eye-level behind a wheel is much lower than when standing, and as you are concentrating on the road ahead your field of vision is much restricted.

Black letters on a yellow ground, black on white or white on black are the most visible. The latter are perhaps more likely to fit in with the colour scheme and image of most pubs. Do not plaster the building with notices. This will only tend to confuse.

The message should be brief and to the point. There is no need to put the name of the pub on every sign. It is already on your swinging sign, and is not generally of immediate interest to someone looking for a pint of real ale or a sandwich, as long as it is obvious that it is a public house. If they are flying by at 50 miles an hour, by the time they have digested the name they may have missed the message. Use short terms, and where possible, evocative ones. For example, 'log fire', or 'hot soup' on a cold winter's day, or 'ice-cold lager' in high summer. Put the most important ones at the top.

My signs were generally written in wetted chalk on a blackboard which had been thoroughly washed off so that no smears remained. This ensured a sharp contrast and the message could be changed at will. The boards were easily and cheaply made from thick blockboard with several coats of matt black paint.

A typical one, with what I hoped and intended would be the impression given to potential customers in brackets, was:

XVth CENTURY INN	(Quaint, cosy, comfortable)
LOG FIRE	(Cosy, warm, homely)
HOME-COOKED FOOD	(Should be good)

REAL ALE   (Traditional, quality)
CHILDREN'S ROOM   (That settles it, We're
stopping here!)

In the summer I would put BEER GARDEN instead of LOG FIRE, and I had a separate sign saying 'Morning Coffee' which could be removed at lunchtime. This, of course, suited a particular kind of pub. Another might have advertised the restaurant, pool table, disco, pizzas or juke-box.

Make sure that your car park is well and clearly indicated. A car driver is much more likely to stop if he can see it in plenty of time, and pull in easily. Remember that he has to notice the pub, be sufficiently attracted by the information on your boards, decide to stop, look for the car park, and turn in—all within seconds.

Eye-catchers
A clean, well cared-for appearance indicates that everything inside will also reflect that care and consideration. A scruffy exterior is off-putting because it suggests that the beer, the food, and the welcome will also be inferior.

There is a lot you can do, not only to make this outer wrapping attractive, but also to catch the eye of passers-by and encourage them to stop. For example, masses of flowers in window boxes, tubs, and hanging baskets dress up any exterior most effectively. Their bright colourfulness gives the impression of a cheerful, welcoming place. But do the job properly. Drooping or dead flowers have quite the wrong effect. Your local nurseryman will probably plant them up for you at a reasonable charge. You must then feed and water them frequently. Hanging baskets in particular should be watered once or twice every day without fail. It is a chore, but one that will be amply repaid by a brilliant, arresting display.

If you have a beer garden, make sure that the tables and gaily coloured umbrellas are visible from the road if at all possible. Well stocked flower borders, neatly trimmed lawns, shady trees will enhance the effect: nothing is more welcoming for a

Running Your Own Pub

hot and thirsty traveller, or for long-suffering parents with fractious children in the car.

Wagon wheels, farm implements, a vintage car, almost anything old and interesting will also draw attention. Use your imagination but remember to make sure that any such attraction is in keeping with the general style and image of the house. My first pub was called the Plough, so I had an old horse-drawn plough set up prominently outside which created endless interest, and was a frequent topic of conversation.

Lighting

That same pub was quite remote, but could be seen from a long way off. I put a soft, warm light in every window, which not only made the place look cosy and inviting close to, but arrested attention more than a mile away.

Lighting, sensitively handled, can have a dramatic effect. It can make your building stand out from its surroundings, while being strongly suggestive of the delights and comfort to be found inside.

Most pubs will not look well in anything too garish, while a plain, brilliant glare, will echo the harsh, monotonous feel of an institution. Go for an exciting, intriguing effect, using a variety of lamps. Create areas of gentle light to bring out features such as the eye-catchers mentioned above, or architectural aspects of the building. Let shadows play their part in creating interest, but make the doorway a welcoming pool of warm light. The interior lighting should also contribute to the exterior scheme by exposing enticing glimpses of the cosily lit bars.

The signs, and the car park, must be lit so as to be easily and instantly visible.

Inside appearance

Your basic policy is particularly relevant in this area. Everything about the interior decor and furnishings should be directed towards the comfort and well-being of your customers. At the same time, every colour you choose, every piece of furniture you buy

60

will be a reflection of your own personality. Your decisions will be made within the bounds of what you think is pleasing. This in turn will have an effect on the type of custom that will be attracted to your pub. They will tend to be, in very broad terms, those with more or less similar ideas to yourself about what constitutes a pleasant and relaxing environment. Thus your customers will not only be affected directly by your personality as it comes over from behind the bar, but also indirectly by its influence upon the building's appearance.

For example, a retired army major whose obsession is huntin', shootin' and fishin' is hardly likely to have a juke-box and a pub full of rocking teenagers. In fact, everything about his place will tend to deter what the landlord would in any case consider to be undesirable custom. They would find little to interest them or to make them relax in such an environment. On the contrary, the lack of loud music, the type of conversation, and the style of decor and furniture would probably make them feel distinctly uncomfortable and out of place.

This is not to say that I would recommend going for just one specific type of custom. Certainly, at one time some landlords would, for example, encourage the so-called 'gin and tonic' trade, and would deliberately discourage others. However, nowadays you need to cast your net much more widely if your bars are to be busy.

Division of space
In many places separate bars have gone out of fashion, perhaps as a result of a revolution in our ways of thinking about social divisions. The old class distinctions have largely disappeared, and it seems only right to sweep away labels such as 'Public Bar' and 'Saloon Bar' with their connotations of 'them and us', the workers and the gentry.

However, in doing so there is a danger of sweeping away something of value. Now that we no longer feel the need to segregate ourselves from other classes, we can more clearly see the advantages, and sheer pleasures, of different kinds of drinking environments for their own sakes, according to our changing moods and circumstances.

For example, if I am out for a drink in male company, perhaps dressed with less than sartorial elegance, and contemplating a game of darts or dominoes, I feel more relaxed and at home in the public bar. There is something reassuring, in fact downright pleasurable, about the solid, unpretentious, unadorned, masculine feel of that traditional drinking environment.

On the other hand, when in more sophisticated mood, the comfort, elegance, and, if desired, greater privacy to be found in the saloon bar may be what I seek.

In any case a very large part of the appeal of a pub lies in the overall atmosphere of homeliness which is partly made up of feelings of seclusion, almost protection. Apart from the often subconscious desire to escape for a while from the outside world, people do not like to feel exposed in a public place. Thus you will see a knot of sunbathers crowded together on an otherwise deserted beach, or the automatic gravitation of drinkers in a bar towards a wall, a corner, or even a post.

Separate rooms therefore have a fundamental appeal, and within them should be subdivisions providing semi-secluded areas or compartments echoing 'caves' in which people can relax and feel secure. By the same token, large areas of empty floor space should be avoided.

At the same time such divisions should not cut people off completely from the interesting and exciting things going on around them. They like to retain a contact with other people, and with the overall ambience of the place, so the boundaries must rather be suggested than actual, and most will not rise much above eye-level when seated.

The corners, alcoves, niches, uprights and pillars already existing in the rooms provide natural starting points for these subdivisions, and can be augmented by intelligent use of bench seating, settles, posts and rails, even plant stands. Changes in the floor level also help.

Avoid any degree of regimentation. Make the boundaries informal, the levels uneven, the furniture differing in style. Neat rows of matching chairs and tables, reminiscent of hospital waiting rooms or school classrooms, will destroy any feeling of relaxed cosiness. The apparent irregularities of the various nooks and crannies thus formed enhance the element of excitement, the illusion of exploration and discovery.

Lighting

Lighting in such places as factories, offices and public buildings is primarily designed to provide the best possible visibility for the people working in them. Naturally your customers need to be able to see what they are doing, but the major function of lighting in a pub is to assist in the creation of that all-important atmosphere.

An artist adds depth, interest and mood to his work by the skilful use of light and shadow, and the same can be done for a bar. Clinical, gloomy or dull effects are caused by the uniformity of the lighting, not by its intensity. Vary that intensity so that shadows are created which define the furniture and decorative features, and the room becomes alive, a place of excitement and exploration.

Bare, visible light sources, and especially fluorescent lamps with their uniform, harsh glare, should be avoided. The aim is to direct white light downwards to form pools on the areas where it is most needed, such as table tops. The polished surfaces of the tables will then reflect that light, breaking it up and spreading it over the mirrors, pictures, brasses, copperware and other warmly reflective surfaces to produce a richly varied, gentle illumination, melting into areas of shadow.

Lampshades are of great importance, not only in directing the light, but also in diffusing and colouring it through the material in other directions. The colours should of course be 'warm', usually those containing red. Pale blues, greys and greens should generally be avoided.

This is not to say that the whole place should be lit by shaded wall lights. Variety and interest can be enhanced by the use of table lamps, standard lamps, pendants, picture lights, even spotlights. There is no need for any of these, including the wall lights, to be all at the same level, or lined up in neat rows.

As a general rule, the eye should not be attracted upwards by ceiling lights. The homely, cavelike feeling is largely destroyed by a bright ceiling, simulating the exposed, unprotected conditions out of doors, and reducing interesting shadow to a minimum.

Walls and ceilings

A warm, homely atmosphere calls for warm colour schemes and the avoidance of large blank or plain areas. Warm colours are generally those with red in them, various shades of brown being particularly useful. Greens, greys and pale blues have a cold, hard appearance, and should be used sparingly, if at all.

Walls should not be too pale, and the large areas of colour should be broken up by pictures and *bric-à-brac*, as discussed below. On the other hand, too dark a colour will look gloomy and not form a satisfactory background. Matt paints will enhance the bald look of a plain colour. Use satin or semi-gloss finishes which, although reflecting the light, diffuse it to produce a softer effect.

Wooden panelling and matchboarding should not, as so often happens, be ripped out (or worse, covered with imitation wood-finish plastic laminate, as I saw in one pub!). This is one of the most sympathetic and most 'pub-like' materials there is. Stripped, stained, grained or painted in natural colours, it will always blend effectively with a homely pub decor.

If a dado exists, keep it. A darker colour up to waist height, blending with that on the upper part of the wall, not only helps to minimise the unsightly results of scuffs, kicks, knocks and spillages, but reduces the plainness while providing a toning background for the furniture.

The eye should not be drawn upwards, towards the ceiling, therefore, unless that large, blank space is already broken up by old oak beams, use anaglypta or embossed ceiling paper painted in dark colours. The higher the ceiling, the darker the colour, as this helps to make it appear lower.

One of the most successful colours is that produced by years of nicotine staining. It has a warmth and glow about it that is highly suitable for pub decor. Match it with your ceiling paint and it will not only look right, but will cause no problems when the nicotine does start to take effect.

Decorations

It has long been something of a tradition to cover walls and surfaces with as many pictures, souvenirs, knick-knacks, curiosities, *objets d'art* and general *bric-à-brac* as possible. It can, I suppose, be overdone, and it does have its critics, but my feelings are generally in favour. It certainly does away with any feeling of bleakness, and provides plenty of interest and variety, supplying endless topics of conversation. It also creates a strong impression, thereby helping to keep the pub in people's minds.

Those items which serve a dual purpose are particularly useful. Brass, copper, pictures and mirrors are effective adjuncts to the lighting scheme. Unusual tables or chairs can also provide interest and a talking point. I had a very handsome Edwardian commode which caused many a laugh and was, at the same time, a popular seat.

Another great attraction in my pub was a selection of snuff on the bar for people to help themselves. This was backed up by pipe-cleaners, spills and matches in the frog (top indentation) of a rough brick on which they could be struck. Many a time customers have told me that they have come back simply because they remembered 'the place with the snuff', even if they did not actually use it. The cost was insignificant, but the consequent advertising spin-off was immeasurable.

Other suitable items are farm implements, old tools, corn dollies, porcelain and china, old posters, badges, weapons, old photographs, especially of the pub or the surrounding district, holiday souvenirs, postcards, models, antiques, unusual bottles, maps and charts, stuffed animals and many more. I used to drink in a pub where the family cockerel would often be seen standing on the bar. Every so often he would electrify the place by unexpectedly crowing. He was a marvellous talking point, and his presence somehow made the house seem friendlier.

A nice touch is to have newspapers, magazines, tourist leaflets and even books lying around for people to browse through. These will encourage them to settle down and stay, and will do your image as a generous and helpful host no harm at all.

Themes
An alternative, and perhaps slightly less cluttered look, can be achieved by a single theme. I know of an excellent pub, for example, near a motor racing track, where pictures and models of cars predominate. This, of course, helps to attract the motoring fraternity, while still providing a pleasant and interesting decor for others. Ships, aeroplanes, hunting, shooting, fishing, horse-racing, dogs, Victoriana and militaria are all good subjects.

You may well have, or may like to start, a collection which could be displayed to advantage, and which, by reflecting your own interests and personality, can help to enhance your role as host. Clocks, beer mugs, badges, theatrical mementoes, weapons, club and old school ties, bottles, and rock and mineral samples come to mind.

Flowers
Do not forget flowers and plants. There is probably nothing else which has such a powerful effect on the mood of the customers and the atmosphere of the pub. If you grow them yourself, or buy them from your regulars' private gardens, the cost need not be prohibitive. Alternatively, nurseries may well give you a good discount in exchange for the advertising value. They do need a certain amount of care, and most plants will need spells of rest in the sun, away from the smoky atmosphere, but it is all well worth while.

A showy flowering plant or, say, a vase of daffodils on the bar, backed up by small sprays on the tables can give a tremendous lift to the dreariest room, but look particularly effective on polished table-tops or reflected in mirrors and gleaming metal. Hanging plants can give interest to odd corners, or help to lower a high ceiling. A display on a window-ledge, seen from the outside, will often be the deciding factor in encouraging a hesitant passer-by to come in.

Notices

May I here make a plea for the banishment of what I call 'no-no' notices? If you are attempting to encourage people to come into your premises, and once there to relax, throw off inhibitions and enjoy themselves, why face them at every turn, and most particularly at the front door with: 'No dogs', 'No children', 'No swearing', 'No food after 2pm', 'No glasses outside', 'No jeans', 'No singing' and so on and on and on? Not exactly welcoming is it?

Be sure, first of all, that the prohibition is really necessary, or that alternative arrangements, such as a children's room, cannot be made. If not, then a polite, personal word is so much friendlier than bald print. But if you must have a notice, then at least be a little more positive, and a little less blunt. For example: 'In the interests of hygiene, and the comfort of other customers, we should be grateful if you would leave dogs outside' or: 'We regret we have no facilities for children. The law does not allow those under 14 years of age on the premises.'

Furniture

I have never understood the urge of many new publicans to spend a fortune ripping a place apart and completely refurbishing and refurnishing at the first opportunity. 'We've got rid of all those horrible nooks and crannies,' one publican told me after utterly ruining his fine old stone-built, oak-panelled Dorset pub. Somehow the chrome, purple plush, garish carpet and wide open spaces would never replace that marvellous, irretrievable ambience!

Running Your Own Pub

Admittedly dirt, gloom, and battered grubby furniture will probably have been keeping custom away, but brand new, expensive furniture, decorations and decor are not necessarily going to produce a better atmosphere. You may well find that a good clean, and the repair of the worst ravages of time revive an ambience merely hidden by years of neglect. The nooks and crannies, the dadoes and friezes, the panelling and matchboarding, and much of the furniture may well hold the secret to a room's basic character. Sweeping all unthinkingly away could well destroy your best chance to re-create a unique and formerly well-loved ambience that, sensitively handled, will regain its deserved popularity. And just think of the money you could save.

I have rarely bought brand new furniture for any of my pubs. In most situations, the older well-made pieces fit in with the general pub image far more naturally than ranks of exactly matching, plastic upholstered, modern furniture. I know of one pub in fact where a great deal of money and designer talent has been spent to ensure that none of the brand new, custom-made tables and chairs look the same!

Local salerooms will often produce items no longer fashionable in private houses, but ideal for pub use, at a fraction of the cost of new ones. I have paid £1.50 for a serviceable and quite elegant table, and as little as 50 pence each for strong pub chairs.

But whether you buy new or old, or simply retain what is already there, you must have an overall pleasing blend, which is mainly a matter of avoiding too diverse a range of styles and colours. For example, a heavily polyurethaned light elm table in a chunky, rough hewn style, will not look well alongside an elegant, hand-polished, antique oak one.

Otherwise a gentle mixture helps to enhance a feeling of informality and homeliness, especially if you can fit in one or two small easy chairs around a low table. In one pub I had a large and deep settee in front of the fire, mainly because it was too big to go up the stairs into the private quarters. It helped immeasurably in creating a cosy atmosphere, and was one of the things that helped in keeping the pub in people's

68

minds. Be careful, though, that you are not using up too much valuable drinking space.

The most important consideration is your customers' comfort, although this does include the pleasing of his eye. The more comfortable he is, the longer he is likely to stay. The longer he stays on your premises, the more money he is likely to spend. (Studies have been made which show that this is generally true.) Try out all your existing furniture, and any you intend to buy, not just for a few seconds, but for five minutes or more. Something that seems very comfortable on first impression can often quickly become otherwise.

Ideally, the height of the seat should be such as to allow the weight of the legs to be borne by the feet firmly planted on the floor, and not by the thighs resting on the chair surface, which, by virtue of the compression of blood vessels and nerves, will rapidly cause discomfort. People differ considerably in size, but a seat height of 40 to 45cm for a dining chair is about right. A lounge seat can be a little lower, say 38cm, as people tend to stretch their legs forward, while still avoiding the pressures mentioned above. Avoid very low chairs as they make for difficulty in rising, and so discourage return trips to the bar.

A reasonable seat width, 45 to 50cm, is desirable, primarily to accommodate the shifting of position which eases a long spell of sitting. Seat depth, to assure a comfortable relationship to the backrest, should be between 40 and 45cm. The backrest should ideally slope at an angle of about 100 to 110 degrees, but it is probably more convenient to judge this by trying it out yourself. In any case, drinkers, especially when engaged in conversation, tend to lean forward, and not use the backrest very much.

Table height for eating in conjunction with a seat height of 40 to 45cm, should be at least 66cm to the under surface to give sufficient space for thighs. Experiments have shown that the ideal height to the table top is 70cm. However, as the traditionally accepted height is more like 76cm, most tables will be too high. This is perhaps not too great a problem, and if all your tables are somewhat higher than the ideal

I would not be unduly dismayed.

Flooring
Do not automatically rush into heavy expenditure on carpeting. Many bars are much the better for a bare floor, with perhaps an odd rug or two. Among my most frequented hostelries are a sixteenth century inn with wide, highly polished, wooden floorboards; a country pub with an old, well-worn wooden block floor laid directly on to sand; another with Cambridge bricks polished and worn by a hundred thousand feet; several typical Dartmoor granite ones with huge slabs of dark, gently glowing slate; a charming village inn with quarry tiles; and an old beerhouse with highly polished lino. In each case the best carpet in the world would not look as good. The surfaces are easily cleaned and will never need replacing. In view of the considerable expense involved, it is worth reflecting upon the number of drinks you will have to sell to recover the cost of your floor covering.

However, if carpet it must be, and certainly it can work wonders in an otherwise cold and dreary room, it is unfortunately true, and not just the salesman's attempt to get you to spend more, that cheap qualities are just not equal to the wear they will receive. However, it is not nowadays always necessary to go for the most expensive. In recent years some excellent commercial quality carpeting has been developed in the medium price range, so shop around.

Anyone who has plain carpets in their home will know why I recommend some form of patterning, but without too many colours, and on the darker side to avoid dirt and stains showing up too much. Vacuum clean them at least once a day, and shampoo them regularly. Commercial machines can be hired very reasonably, and take the hard work out of the job.

Shun the more garish colours and patterns. The decor generally needs to be of a restful nature if the customers are to feel relaxed, and it is easier to tone everything in with a reasonably 'quiet' carpet.

Counter and back shelves

It is important to remember that the bar counter and the back shelves are the shop window of your business, with you at the centre of the scene. Not that I am suggesting that you take the place of the tailor's dummy, surrounded by a glamorous but static display. On the contrary, what should be presented to your customer's eye is more a piece of lively, almost enchanting, theatre with a stimulating backdrop of tempting goodies. Sparkling bottles with their colourful labels, gently glowing dispenser lights, the deep reflections from the counter top, the warm colours of the bar towels, the back-shelf illumination glinting on glass, copper, brass and highly polished wood. Needless to say, dusty bottles, smeared shelves, grimy beer pumps and a sticky bar will not encourage spending; unnecessary clutter such as empty coffee cups, newspapers, transistor radios, half-eaten snacks, full ashtrays, dirty glasscloths and a slovenly, slouching barman will instantly destroy all enchantment.

Aim to make each trip to the bar a pleasurable occasion, a bit of an adventure. Create the desire to 'window shop', to experience the excitement of choosing from an exciting display. Knick-knacks and curios on the back shelves also help in the overall picture you are building, and attract the eye, although if overdone they look confusing, or cause interest to be drawn away entirely from the items you are trying to sell.

Remember your take-away trade as well. While someone is sitting or waiting at the bar, give them the opportunity to be reminded to take home a few cans, a bottle of wine, or a box of chocolates. If you want to sell them, have them on display.

The lighting can make all the difference. The back shelves should be lit from in front using, say, warm coloured spots, directed from a high point downwards. Over the bar you need gentle white light directed straight down and not shining outward into the room. Pools of somewhat greater intensity will be needed over the till and over the drinks preparation areas.

Under-bar lighting is often neglected, but it can enormously simplify washing-up, glass stacking, barrel changing, repairs and adjustments to equipment, and cleaning. All light sources should be hidden from public view.

The counter top must always be solid wood. Plastic laminates *never* look right in a pub. In fact, just the presence of the few square feet needed for the bar can completely ruin all your work in building up a room with the proper pub ambience. It seems that the hard, unyielding, unnatural, almost clinical feel just does not fit in a drinking environment. Also, it will inevitably become scratched, chipped and split in time, and will not withstand cigarette burns: nothing looks more unattractive.

Modern melamine finishes for wood will withstand a tremendous amount of wear, and sanding off and refinishing is not nowadays such a hard job. Just be sure that the finish you use is not one of those with an unnaturally bright, hard gloss.

The counter is also the point of contact between you and your customers. Anything which inhibits that contact, or forms any sort of barrier, will obviously affect the relationship between you. The depth of the counter should not therefore be great enough to cause a feeling of distance. Floor levels on both sides of the bar should be the same if possible, and any objects on the bar large enough to come between you in an obtrusive way should be removed.

Heating

Warmth is so very important. Why landlords expect people to stay in their establishments while they slowly freeze I shall never know. Certainly heating is a very expensive item, but unless you provide the conditions in which customers will choose to stay and spend money, you will never be able to afford it anyway. Cold is the most efficient depressant and cause of bad temper that there is. Everyone, including yourself and your staff, is likely to be miserable. All your hard work in developing a cheery atmosphere goes down the drain.

The system you choose will depend on fuel costs and availability in your area, and on what already exists on the premises. It is well worth going to a lot of trouble to investigate the best method for your particular circumstances, even to paying a heating consultant. Efficient heating can bring about huge savings over the years and have most beneficial effects on your turnover.

I heartily recommend open fires, if only as part of the whole heating scheme. The extra work involved is nowhere near as great as is generally claimed, while the advantages in a pub are very significant. A glowing, flickering fire instantly provides a feeling of cheerful homeliness, as well as giving out a visible, palpable heat which adds immeasurably to one's pleasure.

Music

The provision of music always creates a problem, for you cannot please all of the people all of the time. There is a minority who feel that music in any form is out of place in a pub, and as a customer I tend to agree with them. But the experts generally agree, and certainly experience shows, that background music does have a significant effect in enhancing the ambience you are trying to achieve.

Indeed, I have found that, carefully handled, it can dramatically alter the mood of the place. At lunchtime, and in the early part of the evening, I played light, unobtrusive music which helped conversation along because people were not inhibited by the feeling that others could overhear. It seemed to lift everyone's spirits and lighten the prevailing mood.

However, late on Friday and Saturday nights, when I usually had a house full of 20 to 30 year olds, I played rock and pop music. The louder it was, the more animated they got. They had great difficulty in conversing over the din, but that did not stop them, and they always insisted that they had had a marvellous evening. Certainly my till was happy.

Towards closing time I gradually reduced the volume, finally switching off at 'time'. The atmosphere of excitement I had generated just collapsed, and I usually had no trouble in sending everyone home.

Once again, much will depend on your personal taste, but do not get into the habit of just bunging on any old tape and forgetting about it. Choose your music, and the volume, carefully, according to the appropriate mood and the general type of person on the premises. Avoid having the same artist or the same type of group with a similar basic sound for long periods. After a while it will get intrusive, and eventually annoying. Constantly keep an ear out for the volume in relation to the general level of conversation, and adjust accordingly. As a general rule it is not wise to make it difficult for people to hear one another comfortably.

When buying a music system remember that it is going to be in use for many more hours a day than in even the most devoted music buff's private house. You may feel that the sound quality does not have to be of a particularly high order, but cheap equipment is not generally sufficiently robust to withstand the wear and tear, not to say the dust, smoke and beer spillage, of life in a pub. Ask your supplier's advice.

Juke boxes do have their advantages. After all, it means that the customer pays for the music, but at the same time you have very little control over what is played. Furthermore, adjusting the volume is not usually a very popular move. They really are only suitable if you are mainly concerned to attract young people either to the pub as a whole, or to one particular bar. Even then, a tape player operated by you does mean that those who dislike loud music can be kept happy at those times when the juke-box devotees are not about.

If you do have one, be positive about it and make sure it earns its keep. Do a bit of market research among the regulars every so often. Find out what records they would like, and make sure that the operating company provides them. This ensures happy customers and a full cash box, but see page 131 about copyright.

The traditional form of music in pubs is the good old upright piano. You may well find it worthwhile investing in one, especially if you have a reasonable piano player among your clientele. A good sing-song, perhaps on a regular night, is a great crowd-puller, while just the sight of a piano may well bring about a spontaneous evening's entertainment. Of course a piano can take up a lot of good drinking space, which must be taken into account when weighing up its potential value.

Public bar
I have previously advocated the retention of separate bars. The public bar is such a unique drinking environment that its decor and furnishings have to be treated in a somewhat different manner from the rest of the pub.

Overall, the traditional public bar has a more down-to-earth feel to it. It somehow manages to retain an atmosphere of relaxed homeliness while at the same time displaying a spareness, a simplicity, almost a ruggedness. Much of this may stem from the fact that, originally, working men would be accommodated in the kitchen of an inn, a room at the centre of the home, but at the same time having the characteristics of a place of work.

Subdivision will not be so desirable here because conversation tends to flow around the room, as indeed it would have done in the kitchen. The decor will be warm, but simple and unpretentious, avoiding decoration or the rather cluttered look advocated for other bars. The dartboard, a notice-board, and just a scattering of old advertisements, pictures, and relevant photographs of the regulars and their activities will be sufficient.

Natural materials are perhaps even more important here for they manage to combine a feeling of strength and simplicity with one of warmth and resilience, in keeping with the desired atmosphere. Just because the room is relatively plain and down-to-earth, do not be tempted to introduce modern plastic or chrome substitutes, which instead of mellowing comfortably, simply become tatty and worn. The floor should certainly not be carpeted. Flagstones, wood, tiles or brick are preferable, or well polished

Running Your Own Pub

lino without strong patterns or garish colours, if there must be a covering. Strong, well made, wooden furniture of simple, honest design, such as would be found in a kitchen, is needed. And at least one large sturdy table should be provided for dominoes and card games.

The lighting, while never being harsh, should be somewhat brighter for playing darts and table games, or for reading the paper. Fancy lampshades or exotic lighting effects are not suitable, although light sources should still be hidden. The fittings must be plain and simple like everything else in the room, but nothing should ever be of poor quality or cheap design.

Chapter 5
Drink

Drink is, of course, the subject of your profession. You will be spending your life looking after, and selling the stuff. You should be an expert.

We do not expect a butcher to be ignorant about meat or a solicitor not to understand the law, but many a publican has only the sketchiest knowledge of his merchandise, and much of that founded on folklore and prejudice.

Learn, and keep learning. You will never know all there is to know. You may think you can distinguish between whiskies, but there are 2000 of them. You may be well versed in wine, but can you tell the vineyard from the bouquet? Of course you know beer, but there is always one you have not yet sampled.

Be knowledgeable when approached for advice or information. Be ready when asked for an unusual drink. Know about the right glass, the right temperature, the right mix, the right measure.

It would require several volumes of this size to give you a reasonable knowledge of your subject, and I therefore can only lay a basic groundwork. I recommend first a visit to your local public library where there should be several books on the manufacture, history and care of the various basic drinks. On pages 153-5 you will find a list of recommended reading, and the organisations who can help.

If you are seeking a tenancy it is likely that the brewery will require you to attend a training course. In the meantime, get a part-time job in a nearby pub, and pester the landlord with questions.

But, having rid yourself of folklore and prejudice, do not become the evangelist prepared to sweep away your customers' misconceptions whether they like it or not. Your enthusiasm can just be boring to anyone

77

else. Unless genuinely asked for your expertise, bow to other people's 'superior knowledge'. For there is a lot of snobbery about the lore of drink, and nothing is gained from puncturing someone's self-importance, except perhaps the loss of his custom. If he believes that this well advertised port is superior to that cheaper one, do not disillusion him. Pocket the higher profit and save his ego.

This is not to suggest, however, that you should deliberately mislead, or leave someone in the dark. If you have a genuine enquiry, then it is your duty as the expert in the field, and in accordance with your basic policy, to ensure that your customer has the best advice, and gets the best product for the price. Fobbing people off with second best is a certain way to lose repeat custom.

Beer

There is nothing mysterious about the art of keeping beer. It requires common sense, care, and a pride in the product you sell. There is, however, a great deal of discrimination, discernment, indeed connoisseurship, among serious beer drinkers, and rightly so. The reward for the proper care of beer is not only your customers' approval, but also the fact that if it is good it goes down more easily and more quickly. More of it gets drunk, and they return more often to drink it.

There is an old saying: 'There's no bad beer, only bad publicans.' This is true. If a beer gets an unfortunate reputation you can usually trace the fault back to the people who dispense it.

Real ale

All praise to the Campaign for Real Ale. Not only did they stop the drift away from the many delightfully different and wholly individual beers that were fast disappearing, they also mounted a huge and highly successful public relations and advertising campaign for beer without it costing the industry a penny. Perhaps even more importantly, they ensured that we publicans retained a real skill and a pride in our trade.

Drink

Looking after good beer is not a hard job, and brings real satisfaction, more especially if you drink it yourself. Real ale, or more correctly cask-conditioned beer, is simply that which arrives from the brewery with the full process of fermentation not yet complete. It goes through a secondary fermentation in your cellar.

Ideally, that cellar should be maintained at a constant temperature of 54 to 55 degrees Fahrenheit, 12.5 degrees centigrade. Refrigeration equipment is often installed for this purpose, but many cellars seem to be naturally just right. Although I have, of necessity, served perfectly good real ale from a barrel in the bar, where temperature fluctuation is enormous, there is no doubt that it would have been much improved if maintained at the correct temperature. Many beers would not have survived such conditions at all.

On delivery the cask is laid on its side on a wooden framework called a stillage, and held in place with wedges. It is then left in that position for 12 hours to adjust to the cellar temperature. In the top is a wooden bung with a wood or plastic centre-piece so made that it can easily be knocked through to the inside. This is achieved with a mallet (I always found the hide variety best) and a softwood peg. The softwood is porous. It lets air in and allows the fermenting beer to escape as it froths and bubbles. It may do this instantly, so a certain amount of skill is required to ensure that the peg is driven in hard enough to avoid a fountain—and a soaking—while not so hard that it is difficult to remove when the time comes. Occasionally the peg gets clogged up before fermentation has finished, so check it now and then, and replace if necessary.

Twenty-four hours is an average fermentation period, but some beers will gallop through in four hours, while others may take two or three days. When all activity appears to have stopped, a brass or chrome tap, thoroughly cleaned with a bottle-brush is driven into the bung at the bottom of the cask, knocking the central indented section inwards. This also requires practice.

79

As long as the stillage is the usual type, holding the cask some 6 or 8 inches above the floor, I recommend my rather unorthodox method. Straddle the cask backwards, as though you were about to sit on it (if it is 18 gallons capacity or less) or just rest your behind on a 36-gallon barrel. Bend forward, grasping the tap firmly and keeping your fingers out of danger. Hold it hard against the bung and strike the end vigorously with your mallet, following up if necessary with two or three lighter blows to drive it right home. Any timidity or hesitation will inevitably bring disaster in the shape of a jet of wasted beer.

With this method at least you do not get a soaking if things do go wrong, and as you are not busy dodging the jet you can concentrate calmly on finishing the job properly as quickly as possible. Have the tap slightly open to allow the displaced air to escape outwards, thus minimising disturbance to the beer.

The softwood peg is then removed, and if all activity has definitely ceased (sometimes hammering in the tap will start it off again for a while) then it should be replaced by a hardwood peg to keep out the air until such time as you are ready to dispense. The brewery will supply the pegs.

The beer pipe is then screwed on to the tap, and a fresh softwood peg put in the top to allow air in to replace the beer as it is used. If it is selling fast it may be necessary to leave the peg out altogether. Do not forget to replace it at the end of the session to prevent any possibility of contamination, and to check deterioration.

Some cask-conditioned beers are dispensed by top pressure, instead of the traditional hand pump or the more modern electric pump. In this case the peg is replaced by the metal nozzle of a CO_2 gas system which provides just enough pressure to push the beer up the pipe.

Draw off the first pint or two until the beer is running clear. Sample it yourself before serving. It should be clear and bright, and have no unpleasant taste or smell. If there is any doubt at all about its condition do not, under any circumstances, serve it. It is far better to lose the sale of a pint or two than

Drink

to lose a customer permanently. You may find that it needs to settle a little longer, but if you feel that you have a complaint against the brewery, contact them as soon as possible. They may want to inspect it themselves. They will want to know the gyle (or batch) number which identifies the particular brew. It is usually stamped on a small paper label on the top end of the cask.

Before the cask becomes two-thirds empty it must be tilted forward to ensure that you obtain all the saleable beer. This must be carried out with great care to avoid disturbing the thick sediment at the bottom. The cellar will contain either blocks or a tilt stick to prop up the back end.

Once the cask is empty, hardwood pegs are driven into both bungholes to seal it against contamination. Remove it from the stillage and stack it ready for collection by the brewery dray.

Keg beer
Keg beer has been conditioned, pasteurised and filtered before leaving the brewery. This ensures that it is in perfect condition and ready to serve as soon as it reaches your pub, and has the added advantage of a longer life.

On arrival in the cellar it needs no special treatment, but the casks should be stored in order of delivery so that the oldest is always used first. The cask is a sealed metal container with a single valve at the top. A connector containing both the beer pipe and the CO_2 pipe is easily inserted into the valve by hand. You can begin dispensing right away.

Most keg beers pass through a refrigeration unit, or cooler, so that they arrive in the glass at just the right temperature, regardless of that in the cellar. This means that if space is short, or there is no cellar, the casks can be kept under the bar or in any other convenient space. The cooler, and all of the dispense equipment, will be provided and installed by the brewery, who will also carry out any repairs.

Cleaning
Apart from the care necessary in actually preparing

cask-conditioned beers, the essential factor in the dispensing of a perfect pint, whether real ale or keg, is cleanliness. Yeast, such an important ingredient of that delicious nectar, can also be its worst enemy. So-called 'yeasty beasties' and other bacteria fond of stale beer and dirt, thrive in a dirty cellar, and can swiftly ruin whole casks.

Your cellar must be scrupulously clean, and the beer running from a secondary fermentation must not be allowed to stand. Scrub it down daily with a stiff broom and water. Use a disinfectant without a strong odour as this can affect the flavour of beer.

Yeast is also the main problem in the pipes. As beer passes through, and more particularly when it is static, it leaves yeast particles on the inside. After a few days these will have built up sufficiently to affect the flavour adversely, cause cloudiness, and bring about a slight fermentation which increases froth (or fobbing) to the point where dispense becomes unbearably frustrating, and very wasteful.

Pipe cleaning at least once a week, preferably twice, is essential. This is where the saying about bad publicans, quoted above, is at its most pertinent. Nine times out of ten a bad pint can be blamed on dirty pipes. Never let it happen to you.

There are various cleaning systems and the brewery will advise you about their particular one. Generally, it is a matter of drawing special fluid into the pipes, where it stands for a while loosening the yeast deposits, and then flushing through with clean water.

Bottled beer
Bottled beers are generally easily handled. However, it must be remembered that they do deteriorate in time and it is necessary to rotate your stocks. Organise your bottle store so that the oldest are used first. When refilling the shelves be sure to bring the oldest to the front.

Some beers, particularly lagers, should be chilled. It is essential to have a cold shelf, or at least a refrigerator. The advantage of the former is that your customer can see in advance that you have his favourite drink at the right temperature. Brewers often supply cold shelves at a competitive price.

Dispense

All beers should be dispensed with care. The visual effect is most important as it persuades the customer of the quality of his drink and enhances his enjoyment. You should aim for a bright, clear liquid topped with a thick creamy head. However, in some parts of the country real ale drinkers prefer little or no head. Doubtless they will soon let you know.

A clean glass is essential, not only for the sake of hygiene and appearance, but also because grease will totally flatten a head immediately. Pour carefully, commencing down the side of the glass until you are sure that too much froth will not be produced. This is particularly important with bottled beers. Do not stick the neck of the bottle upside down into the glass, or attempt to pour too fast, however busy you are. Hold the glass by the handle or by the lower half. Never pass it over the bar with your fingers on the rim.

With pint, and where applicable, half-pint glasses, ask whether a straight glass or one with a handle is preferred. Bottled beers should be poured into glasses that are slightly too big in order to accommodate the head. Draught beers must be served in government stamped half-pint or pint glasses, unless dispensed by metered pumps.

Spirits

Spirits are comparatively easy to care for and dispense, and consequently there is a tendency for any old glass to be banged up to the optic and plonked in a take-it-or-leave-it manner in front of the customer.

However, there is a professional way to do it and, as many spirit drinkers regard their favourite brew as the nectar of the gods, albeit served in pitifully small amounts, they feel that every precious drop should receive the loving care it deserves. Do the job properly and you will earn their loyalty, and give yourself professional pride.

Glasses

The glass should be spotless, and of the right size to accommodate the particular drink comfortably, without unduly emphasising the small dimensions of the legally permitted measure. 6⅔-ounce Paris goblets are usually the most suitable for spirits which are to be drunk neat or just with ice, soda or water. Some prefer the more masculine look and feel of a chunky old-fashioned, and it is a good idea to have a few available for such customers.

For drinks with mixers, such as tonic water, bitter lemon or ginger ale, a glass that will take the spirit with ice and the whole of the contents of the bottle is necessary: 8-ounce Paris goblets are ideal, although even the 12-ounce one can be used to advantage as it lends a touch of glamour to the look of a sparkling drink clinking with ice cubes. (Bottled beers look very good, and a little more 'up market' in this glass too.)

Tall straight-sided glasses also show off drinks such as Bacardi and Coke, or some cocktails, to advantage, especially when using straws, swizzle-sticks or parasols. Keep in mind that women generally have smaller hands than men and, also for aesthetic reasons, prefer a daintier glass.

Dispense

It is obvious, therefore, that you must be sure exactly what your customer requires before starting to dispense so that you can select the appropriate glass. If he wants ice, put it in first. As the liquid runs over the cubes it is cooled far more rapidly than if they are dropped in later. It also prevents the possibility of overflow if the glass is fairly full.

If water is required, it is considered by many to be correct practice to put it in for the customer. However, as a whisky-and-water drinker I much prefer to put it in myself, as nobody else seems to get the amount quite right. In any event bring the water jug to the customer. Do not leave him to hunt for it. Be sure that the water is fresh, and the jug clean.

When it comes to lemonade, cola, lime and orange squash much depends on the type of drink being

Drink

served, and the dispensing system being used, but there is no reason why the customer shouldn't be asked how much he would like.

Mixer bottles can be simply left for the customer to pour, or just started as a gesture of politeness. It is not wise to do more as the amount of dilution desired varies widely. Always ask whether a slice of lemon or a cherry is required.

Your main aim should be to find out what your customer wants, to give him precisely that, and to present it as attractively as possible. A good-looking drink seems to taste better, and so encourages repeat orders. One served in the way that he prefers leaves a favourable impression in a person's mind, and helps to persuade him that yours is a pub to come back to.

Wine

At times there seems to be an article on the correct way to store and serve wine in every magazine, and the books on the subject are legion. However, many landlords have so little professional pride that they have apparently not even bothered to glance at any of them. How many times do you see red wine on the cold shelf, white wine nicely warmed, and both only fit for sprinkling on chips?

Wine by the glass

Wine by the glass is a very popular and profitable drink. Wine lovers tend to be fairly discriminating, even at the 'plonk' level. Do not just buy the cheapest available. Try them out yourself, or if you do not trust your own palate, get someone to do it for you. It is not difficult. You do not have to be a wine master to judge the 'drinkability' of a plonk.

Look at it first; it should be clear and bright. Then sniff it—anyone can recognise an unpleasant smell. Then taste it. Does it taste pleasant? Does it go down smoothly without leaving a disagreeable tang at the back of the throat? After your first taste do you want some more? This simple test should at least tell you whether to try it on your customers. Then ask their opinion. They will be flattered, and impressed by

85

your concern for the quality of the products you sell to them.

Shop around. There are a large number of cheap wines on the market, and the quality does not necessarily have any bearing on the price.

Generally, red wine should be served at room temperature. Back-up stocks look good in a wine rack, and draw attention to the fact that you sell wine. White and rosé wines should be lightly chilled in a refrigerator or on a cold shelf. A good method of chilling and at the same time displaying them to the best advantage is in a wooden tub packed with ice.

Wine by the bottle

There is no reason why serving wine by the bottle should be left to the wine bars. In a pub you do not need a wide range, or anything very exotic. A few well-chosen ones covering a reasonable price range will suffice. Include half-bottles and carafes to cater for those who are not in the mood for a whole bottle.

Have clean, well written or printed wine lists readily available, perhaps one on each of the tables usually used for eating. Describe the wine as fully as possible; 'hock' or 'Italian red' will not do. Get the cooperation of your supplier to draw up the list, and learn from him at the same time. Make sure you are at least knowledgeable about the wines you stock.

Staff availability will decide whether you can afford to serve bottles at tables. One advantage is that you can encourage consumption by topping up glasses every so often. However, it is perfectly acceptable in a pub to pass the opened bottle and glasses over the bar, preferably on a tray. For white wine, ice buckets are much appreciated. The metal ones are rather expensive, but there is no reason why you should not use something else. I had some very attractive, simple unglazed earthenware pots, which are actually more efficient at retaining the cold.

Glasses

Paris goblets are very suitable for red wines, and flutes for white. The glass should be big enough to hold your standard measure with plenty of room to spare. On no account should it be filled to the brim. Give generous measures, and if necessary charge a bit more. Nothing looks worse or more mean-minded than a tiny glassful.

Cocktails

For years I would not serve cocktails as I had a vague idea that you had to be an expert, and anyway they were fiddly and time-consuming. Professionalism finally came to the fore. After all, I was supposed to be an expert in my trade, and surely a job worth doing was worth spending a little time and care on.

I soon found that there is nothing difficult or particularly fiddly about cocktails. There is a large demand for them, which is instantly stimulated by the mere fact that they are available. They do take a little longer to serve, but you are selling, and reaping the profit from, two, three or even four drinks in one glass at the same time. When I realised just how much interest there is in them; how they are the perfect thing to offer someone bored with the same old drinks, or uncertain what they want; how they are leapt at, despite the price, by anyone with a reason to celebrate; how the sight of one person's cocktail triggers the desire among others to try them; and how profitable they were; then I kicked myself for not taking the trouble years before.

All you need is a cocktail shaker, colourful 'bendy' straws, plastic swizzle sticks, parasols and some suitably attractive glasses. Choose 10 to 15 recipes which are reasonably simple to put together. Even the more exotic ingredients are readily available nowadays. Make sure everyone knows that you sell them by suitable notices, with tempting descriptions, or cards on each table.

Appearance is all with a cocktail. Be lavish with decorations and garnish, and select those to sell which are interesting and colourful. The parasols, swizzle sticks and cocktail shaker should all be prominently visible on your back shelves. Use the shaker with a flourish thus drawing attention to the fact cocktails are being served. The temptation will be too great for someone.

Soft drinks

Many landlords resent serving soft drinks. One of the more colourful of my acquaintances in the trade tends to say, loudly enough for the embarrassed customer to hear, 'I sometimes wonder why I bothered to get a bloody licence', when a passing motorist orders a tomato juice.

To the professional, however, this attitude is hard to justify. Your basic policy should lead you to happily provide whatever the customer wants, but remember that today's satisfied tomato juice drinker may well be back tonight to have his fill of scotch. And the young lady who always drinks orange juice may only be there because her boyfriend wants to sup a fair few pints. Furthermore, the profit margin on soft drinks is most attractive.

So why not serve them happily and with as much care as anything else? An orange juice served chilled with a slice of orange and a colourful straw is the sort of thing that will help people to remember your pub, and want to come back. Similarly a slice of lemon with bitter lemon or lemonade, or a slice of apple with apple juice, turns an ordinary drink into something special.

There is no reason why you should not be inventive with them, as with cocktails. For example, bitter lemon and orange juice mixed, with lots of ice, a straw and a slice of lemon or orange makes an attractive, refreshing and highly profitable drink. It is called a St Clements (oranges and lemons; got it?).

Cigarettes and tobacco

The profit margin on these items is low, but your basic policy demands that you provide this service, which is expected by a large number of your customers. Pilferage is a problem. One or two missing packets may not be noticed. They are easily concealed and any theft is all but impossible to prove.

Drink

Many packets will have to be sold to recover the loss of each one stolen.

If you are in a position to trust absolutely all those who have access to the stocks, then the personal touch of service over the bar will be very much appreciated. Otherwise cigarette machines are the only safe answer. Shop around for the best commission rates, and be sure that unreliable machines are instantly replaced.

Marketing

To a large extent, of course, a customer does not need to be 'sold' on the idea of a drink. He would hardly be in the place if he had not already decided to buy one. (There is the occasional exception. I once had a chap come in especially to try a pint of 'that Relais Routier you've got advertised outside'.)

Part of the whole picture that you are selling, and in the end the most important part, is the booze. Therefore, as much effort should be put into selling or, more appropriately, marketing your drinks as into everything else. The way in which your wares are presented to the customer is a vital part of a complete package which is designed to make him stay, and to make him come back again and again.

First he must be informed what is available. This is why you have cleverly designed beer pumps on the bar, colourful labels on bottles and eye-catching beer mats and bar towels. Make sure, therefore, that these are used to the best advantage. The back shelf lighting should enhance and clarify the bottle display. The lights on the beer pumps should be working. Beer mats and bar towels should always be clean and fresh.

You can add to what the brewers have already done for you by emphasising those items which not every other pub stocks, those things which are in some way special, different or new, and those which you particularly want to promote.

This can be done in various ways, some of which have already been pointed out. For example, wine in racks and in an ice-packed tub; notices on the walls

89

and on the back shelves; cards on the tables; black-boards; chalked messages on beams; spotlit displays; posters. Your price-list can be displayed in a positive way as an advertisement of your wares, rather than a grubby, barely readable notice grudgingly pinned up in an out-of-the-way place only because the law insists. After all, if you are ashamed of your prices then you are charging too much, and probably turning trade away.

Try to use evocative words such as 'sparkling', 'vintage', 'refreshing', 'mellow' and 'traditional' whenever possible. All notices must be clean and not creased or torn. Handwritten signs done boldly with felt tip pens can be as effective, if not more so, than printed ones. Remember the tip about writing in chalk. The surface should be completely free of smears and the chalk wetted to ensure a sharp contrast.

I am not, of course, suggesting walls plastered with bits of paper, but a variety of methods, taking their place among the other knick-knacks and pictures, will help to add interest to the whole scene.

The appearance of the drinks is also a crucial part of your marketing strategy: a frosted glass of sparkling lager, the deep glow of red wine, the satisfying look of a clear pint topped by a thick head, all enhanced by atmospheric lighting and the gleam of polished wood and metal. Spotless, sparkling glasses help, as do cherries and other fruit, colourful straws, swizzle sticks, ice and parasols where appropriate. A wooden counter-top also makes the best background to show off the colours of the drinks.

It will not hurt to mention special drinks in your newspaper advertising. Cocktails, a particularly popular or unusual real ale, a strong continental lager, or even wine by the glass, will all help to tempt people in.

Buying

Careful buying can make a considerable difference to your profitability, your work load and your peace of mind. Apart from beer which is usually no different

Drink

whether from brewer or agent, price is, of course, usually the main consideration. It is generally true to say that for wines, spirits and soft drinks the brewers are rather expensive. Against this must be set the fact that everything is often delivered in one load with one lot of paperwork.

Wholesalers and agents are often very competitive and have the added advantage of a range comprising several companies' products. Once again it may be possible to have just one delivery, and one lot of paperwork.

Cash and carry warehouses are usually, but by no means always, the cheapest. But your time is precious, and it is easy to spend on petrol as much as you save on the goods.

Your local supermarket is also worth watching. The major brands of gin, whisky, vodka and brandy in particular are often cheaper there than anywhere else.

In practice you will probably find that you have to use all four, especially if you want to offer your customers as wide and varied a range as possible. If this is so then it pays to compare prices. The differences are often significant, sometimes enormous.

Stock cards
The professional way to organise your buying is to have a stock card for each item, with the current price being charged by each supplier noted on it. Each week do a quick stock check so that you can make out your orders simply by going through the cards. In this way you will ensure that nothing is forgotten and that you buy from the cheapest supplier.

The cards also help to prevent running out of stock, which is not only embarrassing and may lead to loss of sales, but also violates your basic policy, as your customer's well-being is hardly being served by the lack of his favourite drink. In fact, it does not take many occasions on which he is unable to have what he wants for him to take his custom elsewhere.

Stock cards will also eliminate unnecessary trips to the cash and carry as it is easier to ascertain how fast each item is selling so that you can buy enough to last

Running Your Own Pub

to the next scheduled visit. They also save a lot of worry at peak times such as bank holidays and Christmas when it is very difficult to judge how much you should order. A quick check back to last year's cards gives an invaluable guide.

I suggest using the common 5 × 3 inch lined cards with the product name and container capacity at the top. For example:

> *Blogg's Best Bitter* 18 gallons
> or *Smith's London Gin* 1 litre

The vertical columns should show the week-ending date. The horizontal ones show the stock at stock-taking time, the amount delivered as per the delivery notes, and the total of the two. At the next weekly stocktake it is simply a matter of deducting the new figure from the old total to see how much you have used, and to calculate what you should order.

Sometimes filling in the cards may seem a bit of a bind, but the saving of time, worry, mistakes and money over the years is incalculable. Moreover, as shown in Chapter 7, such a system has other invaluable uses besides buying.

Discounts and promotions

Quantity discounts are often offered, especially before Christmas and at the beginning of the summer season. These are usually well worth taking for faster selling lines if you have the cash available, or if overdraft charges are not going to eliminate the extra profit. Avoid buying large quantities of a new product, however attractive the promotional offer. In fact it is usually better to leave well alone until customer requests begin to give you some idea of the sales potential. There must be millions of pounds' worth of unsold 'new' products lying in pub cellars that died a death as soon as they were launched, despite the initial ballyhoo.

Equipment

In my opinion, your initial reaction when considering buying bar equipment should be 'no'. For some reason

Drink

the prices for such items, possibly as a result of the popular view that all landlords are fabulously wealthy, seem to be iniquitously high. Furthermore, serious reflection often reveals that the equipment is not really necessary in the first place.

Optics, saving incalculable time, spillage and tempers are worth every penny. Cocktail shakers really do cover their cost. Ice makers are more or less essential in a really busy pub, but hardly justified where a dozen or so trays in the freezer compartment will suffice. A cold shelf or at least a refrigerator is essential, but then a second-hand one can often be picked up at low cost.

I find it very hard to justify a glass washer. The cheaper ones do not make washing any easier or quicker, and with modern glass detergents, no more hygienic. They do not save wages, as in most pubs staff have enough time to wash as they go along, with or without a machine.

The fully automatic ones are a different matter of course, but the high capital cost can only possibly be justified where staff are constantly too busy serving to keep up with the demand for clean glasses.

Draught lemonade and cola machines, with their high profit margin, can be worth while, but check your figures very carefully before splashing out if your sales of those items are not particularly high.

All told, resist rushing into the purchase of high cost machines and equipment, however tempting they may be. Settle into your pub first, and run it without the benefit of such items. Before purchasing, be quite certain that it will really save time or money, or will significantly improve the service to your customers. Think in terms of how long any savings made will take to recoup the initial cost, or how many drinks you will have to sell to pay for a machine that does not pay for itself.

Chapter 6
Food

It is almost entirely true to say that nowadays, any pub where the landlord expects to make a reasonable living must provide at least some food.

I think it is important to remember that you are running a pub and not a restaurant. Your business is booze. It is often said that the catering side of the business is the profitable side. Unless you have a restaurant, I believe that this is no longer true. Admittedly, the gross profit margin is higher, but a round of drinks needs little preparation or costly equipment, causes no great problems of supply or storage, and can be served in seconds. A meal requires far more capital outlay, planning, preparation, fuel, staff and sheer hard work. Furthermore, pub food is generally expected to be cheap. Its saving grace is that it is served and consumed on premises paid for, lit and heated by the drinks side of the business.

Food should be regarded as a way of attracting extra custom, as an advertisement for your establishment. For this reason it should be good and reasonably priced. And this is also why it is nowadays essential.

Fortunately, there is a place for all types of pub catering, from a cheese roll served in a paper napkin to a full à la carte restaurant. Consequently, however humble your skills, you need have no fear that you cannot provide good, satisfying pub fare at some level, for there is nothing mysterious about cooking. All you need is common sense, care and organisation.

The most vital consideration is quality. The thing that brings people back, time and again, to eat at a particular pub is not so much low prices, or an exotic menu, or even the pretty waitress. It is simply good food. A lovingly prepared hamburger containing

94

high quality ingredients is, at the right time, just as important as a soufflé.

At one time I had a good lunch-time trade, served from a fairly sophisticated running buffet, backed up by a wide range of hot dishes. My only real rival was a tiny village pub where a limited menu of sandwiches, hamburgers, ploughman's lunch and pâté was served. He was packed every day, mainly with the type of businessman who at other times entertained clients in my expensive restaurant. His secret was simply the *quality* of the food he offered. So pitch your fare at the level at which you feel competent to provide, without compromising your standards, and look constantly for ways in which you can improve quality.

Market research

Before going into your pub have a look at what is being offered in the area, and see if there is a niche for you to slot into. Try to assess whether your customers will be there because they have got to eat somewhere, as is the case with factory workers or passing motorists at lunch-time, or because they are eating out as an occasional treat, and will therefore need something a little special.

Keep the research going once you are in the pub. Ask your customers what they think of your menu, what else they would like to see on it, and what would bring the family and friends out to eat.

Supplies

The quality of your finished product depends to a very large extent on the quality of the ingredients that go into it. This means buying the very best, even if higher costs force up your prices a little, although it by no means follows that the top price ensures the best goods.

Before rushing off to the cash and carry, or ordering from the big distributors, check your nearby shops. Fresh locally baked bread, rolls, pies and pasties, locally grown vegetables, fresh fish, locally killed meat, and your butcher's prize-winning sausages will often be of high quality, and earn your customers' loyalty. Furthermore, small businesses are usually pleased to have a sizeable pub order, and are therefore willing to give a discount, will be happy to satisfy your special requirements and will do their best to assist in times of emergency.

Do not overlook the local part-time suppliers either. By these I mean the housewife who cooks delicious pies or gateaux, the gardener who often has a surplus of fresh vegetables, or the early riser who comes in with baskets of wild mushrooms. The best pâté I have ever tasted came to me from a dental technician at very reasonable cost, and I have often been supplied with fish, venison and game by local sportsmen.

Of course, you will need to use the large distribution companies, and many of their products are of high quality. Find out which ones deliver in your area through the Yellow Pages, or just by keeping an eye out for their vans. Many huge companies will be quite happy to serve you, however small your order. They are generally more expensive than the cash and carry, but this has to be set against convenience and transport costs. Some items may be even cheaper at your local supermarket.

Always be choosy about what you buy. You have no reason to accept produce that is not of a high standard. Once you get a reputation for being fussy your suppliers will make sure you get the best. It won't do you any harm among your customers either.

Portions

Your basic policy demands the high quality already stressed, but your customer's well-being also calls for generosity on your part, and a willingness to provide what he wants.

This means, basically, big portions, and the provision of the extras that can make a snack into a feast. Take a ploughman's lunch for example. Cut a fresh, crusty, cottage loaf into four, marry a portion to a pot of butter, a man-size chunk of good tasty cheese,

Food

lashings of pickle and an attractive salad garnish. Then you will have a meal that will make your reputation and bring them back for more. Your costing will be higher than if you reduce quantities to the bare minimum, but as long as your customer feels that he is getting value for money, then he will happily pay the extra, and return again and again.

One of my former favourite pubs (I seem to have a lot of favourite pubs!) changed hands some time ago. The new landlord had been a lecturer at a catering college, but he produced such a mean and tired looking plastic-wrapped ploughman's lunch that I have not been back since. (Notice, by the way, how fickle the public can be. Just one bad experience and you lose them forever.)

And give them what they want. How many times have you been told, for example, 'We don't serve chips with steak and kidney pie,' when the chap on the next table is having them with his plaice. As long as you've got them, why not let the customer have them?

It is the same with condiments and sauces. If someone wants to put tomato sauce on the boeuf bourguignon that's his business, but do not leave the hassle of getting it to him. Preferably make it, and the other condiments, available on the table, or on a side table, so that he does not have to ask. If not, then ask him what he wants when you serve the meal.

Don't begrudge the cost of sauces and condiments. They often make a meal come alive (to me a beef sandwich is not a beef sandwich without horseradish) and customer satisfaction must outweigh the few pennies involved.

Menu

So what are you going to put on the menu? First of all consider the things that require absolutely no cookery skill at all and can be put together by minimally trained staff: sandwiches, rolls, pork pies, pâté, smoked fish, ploughman's lunch, seafoods and salads. Then the next stage, those bought-in items that only need heating up: pasties, pizzas, all sorts of

Running Your Own Pub

pies, sausage rolls and toasted sandwiches. Next those meals, bought-in or cooked yourself, which only need the addition of vegetables or chips, such as sausages, faggots, beefburgers, chicken, scampi and pies. Then there are, believe it or not, a limited number of ready-cooked frozen meals on the market that really are good, and which can be heated up by microwave or boil-in-the-bag. Inferior ones should be absolutely discounted, but shopping around will produce a few that you can serve with confidence. Look out particularly for some of the smaller companies that are beginning to appear nowadays, supplying absolutely first-class products with a recognisable home-cooked touch.

A very comprehensive menu can therefore be put on without any real cooking on your part whatsoever. If you have the skill to turn out your own dishes, at least to the extent of following a recipe in a book, then you are one jump ahead.

Delicious desserts can also be easily put together: ice cream, tinned and fresh fruit with cream, banana split, pear Belle Hélène, peach Melba, trifle and even knickerbocker glory. There are plenty of ready-made gateaux, flans and fruit pies on the market, and often available also from your local baker. If you can cook your own you will find many of the old favourites, such as steamed puddings, crumbles and fruit pies, very popular.

Range

It is desirable to have a reasonably comprehensive menu in order to cater for as wide a range of tastes and moods as possible. However, beware of overdoing it. A huge list instantly suggests that only frozen dishes are being served, and anyway, people do not like to be overwhelmed with choice. In any case it is unlikely to be commercially viable in view of the probable waste, the need for large areas of expensive refrigerated storage, and the possible confusion among preparation staff. Quality is always infinitely preferable to quantity.

On the other hand, modern equipment does mean that a reasonable range is feasible. Both bought-in dishes, and those cooked by you, can be defrosted and re-heated in a microwave or forced convection oven. Do not forget, however, that food cannot be safely kept for long periods, even in a freezer, and that refrigeration costs money.

Decoration

How often have you said, 'That looks nice,' when you see a particularly tempting plate of food? You have not even tasted it, but have already decided that it will probably taste good. This means that you are already half won over to the dish before you start, and that the initial appearance is what will probably stick in your memory after the event. How each plateful looks is vital. Use garnishes such as tomato wedges, lemon slices, sprigs of parsley, watercress, mustard and cress, lettuce leaves and cucumber. Even humble sandwiches or pasties can be greatly improved, and a crunchy lettuce leaf helps the taste along too. But watch the prices of these items. The seasonal differences are enormous, and can creep up on you unnoticed.

Think 'colour', not just with garnishes but also with the vegetables you use. Green peas, yellow corn, orange carrots, red capsicums all help to brighten up a dish. Avoid heavily patterned or strongly coloured crockery, as the plate is the background to the food and must not clash or detract from it. Needless to say, it should be spotlessly clean and free from chips or cracks.

Description

A temptingly descriptive menu will also help to make the mouth water. It can be overdone. 'Dew-kissed strawberries' or 'sun-drenched peaches' produce more mirth than appetite, but the word 'bread' makes much more of an impact combined with adjectives such as 'crusty' or 'locally baked', for example. 'Fresh', 'hot', 'tasty', 'delicious', 'tangy', 'crunchy', 'home-cooked' and many more help to stimulate the imagination.

Service

Those who serve the food should be just as caring, responsive and eager to please as the bar staff. Teach them to anticipate the customer's needs, to smile and make sure that he has everything he wants. Let them show by their greeting and the way they put the dish on the table and check for the cutlery, napkin and condiments, that his welfare is important to them.

Many waiting staff wear a mask of stand-offishness or indifference simply because underneath they are shy, even nervous. Explain that in the light-hearted atmosphere of your pub there is no need to fear a customer's reaction. On the contrary, their open friendliness will elicit a similar response, and, indeed, will make a disagreeable attitude far less likely. Let them see that they, being actually in contact with the public, are a very important part of the organisation, and that their skills are of great value.

They should understand that they are members of a sales team who can have a considerable effect on your business, not only by their attitude, but also by their enthusiasm for the product. I have many a time, for example, overcome the reluctance of the figure-conscious to spoil themselves with a dessert by pointing out that the apple pie is *home-made* with *real cream*, or by describing in irresistible detail some luxurious confection.

Your staff should always be immaculately clean, and their clothes and aprons free of stains or grubby marks. Hands and fingernails are of particular importance when handling food.

Do not allow bar staff to serve meals. Apart from the fact that they may not be properly trained for the job, their place is behind the bar, ready to serve drinks, at all times.

Food orders

It is, however, usual for bar staff to take orders for food and, in most cases, to take payment. A good system is therefore essential to prevent delay, mistakes and loss of money.

Use the little, unprinted waiters' pads with an original and one carbon copy. The customer's location is written at the top, facilitated by numbering the tables in sequence around the room. The order should be written clearly with a line drawn right across the page between the separately served courses. Abbreviations or initials may be agreed with the kitchen staff to save unnecessary writing. The figure below shows a complete order and its explanation.

On the kitchen wall is a rectangular board with nails driven in at evenly spaced intervals. The top copy of the order is impaled on the next vacant nail so that the kitchen staff know in which order to prepare the meals. As each order is completed the ticket is taken down, and may be used for kitchen record purposes. For example, a count can be made of the number of portions sold of each dish. You can then check whether the correct portion size is being served, or whether food is disappearing into staff shopping bags.

A typical food order and its explanation

Order		Explanation
3		Table number
2 Tom soups	1.10	First course —2 Tomato Soups
1 PL	1.35	Second course—1 Ploughman's Lunch
1 S+K	2.10	1 Steak and Kidney Pie
1 Van	.50	Third course — Vanilla Ice Cream
1 A Pie	.85	1 Apple Pie
	5.90	

Ideally, the food should be paid for at the bar as it is ordered. The carbon copy is then impaled on a spike, both to show that it has been paid and to preserve it for checking the till at the end of the day. If for some reason the money is not collected at the time, the copy should be kept separately until the bill is cleared, preferably on a nail board similar to that in the kitchen. It is then possible to see which bills remain unpaid at a glance.

It is easy to over-react to the problem of unpaid bills, but let us get it into perspective. I have sold literally thousands of meals, but have only lost out on three occasions, with a grand total of £12.50. I am not at all sure that they were the result of dishonesty so much as sheer forgetfulness. The vast majority of people are honest. One chap went out without paying, and *ten months later* flagged my car down in the road. He not only settled up but insisted on paying interest.

A good system and a sharp eye will usually prevent such incidents. Harassing people for payment because of exaggerated fears does not fit in with a relaxed atmosphere, and may, by discouraging custom, lose a lot more in future business than the price of that one meal. If you feel that someone is about to leave without paying, for whatever reason, a direct, polite approach such as, 'May I take for the meal?' is all that is needed.

Equipment

Once again, I suggest that you do not rush out immediately to spend money on filling your kitchen with shiny new equipment. See how your menu develops first, and be absolutely sure that any apparent need is justified. Weigh carefully the costs of machine versus human being and be satisfied that the quality of your product, or the margin of profit, really is being improved. You have to sell a tremendous number of bar snacks to recover the cost of most appliances.

Catering equipment works much harder than in domestic kitchens, so ensure that anything you do

Food

buy is strongly built. Items specially made for commercial use are usually preferable, although very much more expensive. Over the years, for example, it may be more cost effective to replace domestic-type refrigerators than bear the initial high capital cost of a commercial one. However, such items as pots and pans, and tools such as knives, ladles, scoops and tin-openers should always be of commercial quality.

What you choose is largely a matter of personal taste and your particular situation, but a few general points, gleaned from years of hard-won experience, are worth making.

Stainless steel and ceramic tiles make the best surfaces.

Smoke and fume extraction is vital.

A double oven is a life-saver.

Have two deep fryers so that chips can be fried separately. (Always use long-life oil, it is cheaper in the long run.)

You will need to keep many foods separate from others in refrigerators. Butter, for example, quickly absorbs a taint. It is in any case more convenient and efficient to keep different types of food in different refrigerators, or at least in different compartments: meat in one, dairy products in another, desserts in a third, and so on.

Make sure you have sufficient provision for keeping plates hot.

Never serve hot food on a cold plate.

Double sinks and double drainers make life much easier.

Have plenty of space set aside *only* for stacking dirty dishes and make good, easily accessible provision for plate scraping.

Get advice from your local fire brigade about fire-fighting equipment, and make sure everyone knows how to use it. A fire blanket is invaluable.

Hygiene

I hope it is quite unnecessary to emphasise hygiene. Dirty pub kitchens always become the subject of local

Running Your Own Pub

gossip and quite lurid tales, quite apart from the inevitable effect on the quality of the food. The law is quite severe on this point, and the local Environmental Health Officer will visit you frequently, and will take drastic action if he feels you are not trying to maintain reasonable standards. Prosecutions are well reported in the local press, but this is one sort of publicity you could do without.

Develop habits of cleanliness right from the start. Daily and weekly routines are the only way to ensure that cleaning is done, and done properly. All surfaces, appliances, tools and pans should, of course, be thoroughly washed every time they are used. Refrigerators need a weekly wipe over inside with bicarbonate of soda. Floors should be mopped after each session, and scrubbed by hand at least once a week. Do not neglect walls and ceilings. A frequent wash saves a really tiresome job in the long run. Never allow dirt to build up anywhere. The longer it is left, the harder it is to remove.

Aprons and overalls should be changed daily. You may consider it worth hiring these items, or having your own laundered. Otherwise it is worth investing in a good automatic washing machine and having a routine daily wash.

There are many commercial cleaning aids on the market, most of which are excellent and reduce the work load considerably. But do not be tempted into buying vast quantities, however good the deal may be, or however effective the product seems in demonstration, until you have thoroughly tested it yourself and are satisfied that it really does the job claimed for it.

Chapter 7
Finance and Accounting

The time spent keeping accounting records is often resented: a lot of fiddly figure work just to keep the tax inspector and the VAT man happy, and to give you the privilege of handing over large sums of money to them. Certainly, this was the way I felt in the early days until my accountant pointed out that the accounts were in fact primarily designed to help *me*, not various government departments.

After all, money is what business is about. It is the lifeblood of your enterprise, and unless you are fully aware how and where that lifeblood is flowing, then you cannot claim to be in control of your financial performance. On the contrary, you will be floundering around in the dark, unaware that disaster is just around the corner, or alternatively, that a healthy business is developing nicely. You will not know whether you can afford to carry out improvements or even whether you can survive the quiet winter months.

Accounting records are an invaluable tool which should be used to keep a constant check on how your business is doing. Problems can be anticipated and prepared for, profitability can be monitored, spending checked and your money put to the best use.

The accounts

It is of the utmost importance, in your own interest, that your records should be accurate. It is not difficult, requiring a very basic mathematical ability, and only the cheapest calculator! The big secret is to do them regularly. Never get behind or you will never catch up, and will tend to forget vital points. Once

105

that has happened then your records become useless to you.

The till

Modern tills can be very sophisticated, and very expensive. You will probably be taking over perfectly adequate equipment. I advise you not to rush into replacements, however attractive, and however useful they appear to be. You can so easily end up paying large sums for facilities that are in fact useless to you. The only capability really needed is some form of recording the sales total, which even the most basic ones generally have. Otherwise stick to what you've got until you are sure that you need something better. Tills only take money, they don't make it.

Cash up without fail every day, either last thing at night or, as I did, first thing in the morning when my head was clearer. The previous morning you will have put a 'float' in the till: that is sufficient notes and coins of each denomination to ensure that you have enough change for the day's business (see page 44). You may well have to top up the float during the day. If you do, you must make a note of what you put in, as you will in fact be adding to your float, or you must take out an equivalent amount in another denomination. For example, if you put in a £5 bag of 10-pence pieces, take out a £5 note and put it in the safe, not in your pocket where it may get forgotten and throw out your figures.

Cashing up consists of counting all the money in the till, and deducting the day's float. The balance is the amount of money you took, your 'takings' for the day. You will need to know how much is a result of bar sales, and how much is food. You can either have separate tills, or keep a copy of each food bill to be totalled at the end of the day. Many modern tills have facilities for entering different items separately. A new float is then put in, and a note kept of the amount.

Do not get into the habit of paying small cash accounts or casual wages directly from the till. It is meant to take money, not shell it out. Such practice is bound to get your calculations in a mess. And never

Finance and Accounting

take out pocket money for yourself. Not only will this cause confusion, but if your staff see you do it they may well follow suit.

The books
You will need an analysed cash book. The one I always used was the Simplex Licensees' Account Book published by George Vyner Ltd and available from most good stationers. It is specially designed for pub accounting, and sets out the system so clearly that even I understand it.

The day's takings are entered in the cash book under 'Liquor and Tobacco' and 'Catering', and the total shown. As the bills come in they are entered in the invoice register, and as they are paid they are entered in the cash book under 'Payments'.

At the end of the week (Sunday morning is best because you have a bit more time before you open) all the takings, all the payments and all the money taken to the bank, are totalled in the appropriate columns. Cash and cheque payments are shown separately. It is then a simple matter to carry out a cash reconciliation by counting all the money you have on the premises, including cheques, and comparing the total with the 'Cash in hand' column. Any differences will be the result of a wrong calculation, money genuinely lost, or possibly a hand in the till. Very small amounts can generally be ignored, but frequently recurring or large shortfalls should definitely be investigated.

A bank reconciliation can also be done, which checks that your figure work is correct and helps you to monitor your bank balance.

As mentioned above, all the bills are entered in the invoice register as you receive them. It is important to get an invoice for everything you buy, even odd items from local shops, preferably showing VAT. If for some reason it is not possible or is forgotten, make out a dummy invoice yourself to keep the record straight. Keep the register scrupulously as it is of great help when working out your quarterly VAT return and your gross profit percentage, which I will discuss later.

107

Cash flow

The cash flow projection drawn up on pages 36-7 should be kept going. It will now become one of your most useful accounting tools.

The figures in your cash book can be totalled at the end of each month and used to check just how accurate your estimations in the projection were. If the differences are large you may want to investigate the reason, and you will have to adjust your figures for the coming months.

In any event, this system will tell you whether your closing balance is much higher or lower than expected. If it is higher and continues that way for some months, then by extending your projections you can see whether the surplus will be needed to tide you over the next quiet patch. If it is not, then you know that you will have spare money hanging around which is not working for you, and for which you will have a much better use.

If the closing balance is lower than expected, your figures will show in which area there is a difference between what you expected and what actually happened. For example, it may be that you have spent more on wages than you had budgeted for, or perhaps the electricity bill was higher than estimated. Investigate the point to see whether anything can be done about it. Do you really need so many staff? Can you economise on electricity?

Now amend your projection in the light of these new facts and you will be able to see whether they are likely to cause real problems in the future. By extending the projection it will become clear whether those problems are likely to become permanent, or whether overdraft facilities will tide you over until the situation rights itself. With this forewarning you can see your accountant for his advice, and go to your bank manager for help.

For this reason always treat your bank manager as your business friend and confidant. Keep him in the picture at all times so that he is well armed with the facts when you need to seek his advice or help. Make a point of seeing him regularly, even if things are going well, with the up-to-date situation. His time

Finance and Accounting

costs you nothing, but his advice may be invaluable.

In particular, never get overdrawn without seeing him first, preferably in plenty of time, and after showing him, with the help of the cash flow projection, why and for how long the facility is needed.

Stocktaking and profit margins
In the busy life of a publican paperwork must be kept to a minimum, but there is one other accounting tool which is essential for the proper control of your business, and that is your profit margin. The first step in the calculation is a stocktake. At the end of your financial year you will have to do one so that the accountant can draw up the annual accounts, but for your own purposes of financial control you should aim at a check every quarter.

I have already discussed a quick weekly stocktake in Chapter 5, but as this is only to facilitate ordering, complete accuracy is not terribly important. Your annual and quarterly ones must be as precise as possible, otherwise the information they can provide will be useless, if not downright misleading.

Whereas for ordering purposes it will be sufficient to know that you have roughly two and a half barrels of lager left, or six bottles of a particular whisky, for these checks you will need to calculate down to the last half-gallon of beer, and the last tenth of a bottle of spirits. Bottles will have to be judged by eye, but beer casks can be checked by a special measured dipstick which can usually be obtained from the brewery.

It will be convenient to use the same stock cards however, especially if they contain the latest cost prices, exclusive of VAT. It is then a fairly simple matter to work out the value of each item in stock at the end of the quarter and make a grand total.

This figure can then be used to work out your profit margin. Total the sales income for the quarter, exclusive of VAT. Do the same for the cost of purchases, also exclusive of VAT, using the invoice register which shows the stock actually received in the period. Check back to your last stock figure, or your

109

Running Your Own Pub

opening stock if this is your first quarter, and note the difference between that and the new one. If the new one is greater then the difference must be deducted from the cost of purchases; if less then the difference must be added on. This final amount is then deducted from the sales income to give you the gross profit for the quarter in cash. Multiply that figure by 100 and divide by the sales income to derive the gross profit percentage. For example:

	£
Last quarterly stock figure	2,000
Present quarterly stock figure	2,150
Difference—greater by	150
Total purchases for quarter, excluding VAT	5,350
Deduct stock difference	150
	5,200
Total sales income for quarter, excluding VAT	8,000
Deduct purchases less stock difference	5,200
Gross profit	2,800

$$\frac{\text{Gross profit}}{\text{Sales income}} \times 100 = \text{Profit margin}$$

$$\frac{2800 \times 100}{8000} = 35\%$$

Thus in this particular example the profit margin for the quarter is 35 per cent.

When you have been trading for a while you will know by experience whether this margin is about right for your business. At first, however, you will have to find out by looking at your predecessor's figures, asking your accountant, your fellow publicans or the local branch of the Licensed Victuallers'

110

Finance and Accounting

Association whether it is more or less par for the area.

If there is a significant difference then there may be a problem which needs investigating. A high margin can only really mean that your prices are higher than average. If the customers are rolling in quite satisfactorily then there is no need to change things, but if not you may feel that lower prices will stimulate trade.

A low margin can mean one of several things. It may simply be that your prices are too low, which is easily checked by a quick local pub crawl. Otherwise it may be that either cash or stock is disappearing.

If it is cash it may show up in differences between the amount shown on the till roll and that actually in the drawer at the end of the day. However, dishonest staff need simply not ring up a round occasionally, or ring up an amount less than the actual price and pocket the difference. Another favourite trick is to treat all their friends at your expense.

Missing stock is even harder to trace. If actual bottles are disappearing this can be checked by counting the empties, although it has been known for people to get around that by simply replacing a full bottle with an empty one. If you are fairly certain that someone is 'on the fiddle' then it is mainly a matter of keeping your eyes open, locking everything away that is not needed at the time, and checking all possible areas of temptation. The fact that you are obviously suspicious may have some deterrent value.

Do not forget that stock can disappear in other ways. Spillage, leakage and especially carelessly poured draught beer can mount up considerably. Watch out for brimming drip trays, and for signs of leaks in the cellar. One landlord spent months trying to trace his stock losses only to find that mice had nibbled minute holes in the plastic beer pipes!

Finally, this *actual* profit margin percentage can now be used to correct the estimations in your cash flow projection. It means that you have a more precise way of monitoring your financial performance.

Value added tax

Where annual turnover exceeds £20,500 (1986; the threshold figure is set in each year's Budget) you will have to register for VAT, so it is wise to do so before you take over the pub, first because you will have more time to get to grips with the system, and so will be fully organised to cope with it right from the start. Second because you will almost certainly be paying bills in connection with your future business on which you will be able to claim VAT back. So start right now collecting invoices for any expenses you incur.

To register you will have to contact the local Customs and Excise office who will send you the necessary forms and regulations. You must furnish a return every quarter and pay any VAT that you owe. This is easily calculated by working out the tax due (the current standard rate is 15 per cent) on the total takings for the quarter (you are not likely to be selling any exempt items), known as the outputs, and deducting from that the VAT charged to you on the invoices you have received, the inputs. Your account book is a great help as it is only a matter of adding up the VAT column of the invoice register and the totals of the takings in the cash book. You will not be able to claim the full amount on items such as petrol, which are partly for private use. The VAT office or your accountant will advise on this.

An officer of Customs and Excise will call by appointment every so often to check that your returns are being correctly completed. He will want to see your account book and all your invoices. It is important, therefore, to keep each quarter's papers neatly together, and to keep your records up to date.

Wages

Minimum rates of pay and terms and conditions of service for the trade are fixed by wages councils. The local wages inspectorate will send you leaflets outlining them for each category of staff. These leaflets must be available for your employees to see. There is

Finance and Accounting

nothing to stop you paying over the minimum rates.

Keep a 'signing-in' book where each employee notes his time of arrival and departure. The pay due to him each week is then easily calculated and noted in a wages book which can be obtained from any stationers. An itemised pay statement must be given to all employees who normally work 16 hours or more a week, but it seems wise to do this for everyone who works for you.

The Collector of Taxes will send you the necessary forms and tax tables to make and send on the appropriate PAYE and National Insurance contributions. However you do not have to make these deductions for part-time staff whose weekly wage is below £34 (1984 rate; the level is set in the annual Budget). Your accountant will know the current threshold, or you can check with the local Inland Revenue office.

Your own wage level is, of course, decided by you. Fix a set weekly amount which you feel will be adequate for your needs, and resist the temptation to dip into the till if you are running short at the end of the week. Obviously, too high a figure puts your profits at risk, as your cash flow chart will tell you, while an unrealistically low one can have adverse effects on your own morale. Enter the amount as it is taken under 'Personal amounts withdrawn' in the cash book.

Insurance

You are required by law to insure your employees and to have public liability insurance in case of accident or illness among your customers. If you are a tenant, the brewery will probably insure the building, but you should have cover for furniture, fittings, stock and personal belongings. Insurance against loss of business is invaluable as it ensures an income should trading be interrupted by fire or accident. You should also invest in a retirement pension through an insurance company.

Several companies now offer an insurance package to cover all the aspects you might reasonably require. This certainly simplifies matters, and is usually cheaper than separate policies. Shop around, as rates do vary considerably, or contact a broker. As one who has suffered I strongly recommend approaching only *bona fide* members of the British Insurance Brokers' Association.

Office organisation

You must have a separate area or, ideally, a separate room for your paperwork. The only way to keep abreast of it all is to be well organised. A desk or table should be reserved and not used for any other purpose. Buy wallet files and keep them in alphabetical order in a suitable box or drawer. File everything as soon as it is finished with.

Deal with all outstanding matters every day and do not let yourself get behind. You will never find the time to catch up and there is nothing worse than the thought of a growing pile of paper hanging over your head.

Chapter 8
Staff

In Chapter 1 we saw that the atmosphere of the pub relies heavily on the professional way in which the landlord sets about the job of caring for his customers. It follows that an important part of your job is to make certain that your employees have the personality, the enthusiasm and the training to ensure that your basic policy will be adhered to at all times.

This brings us up against the problem of maintaining that relaxed, easy-going informality in front of the public, while keeping order and discipline behind the scenes. My experience is that the people who care about the welfare of others, and are able to project a genial attitude are nearly always the ones who also bring a sense of responsibility to the job, and therefore cause their employer the least problems. In other words, what you need to look for when taking on staff is self-discipline allied to a cheerful and open disposition.

Engagement

In all but the largest and busiest establishments most employees will be part time or casual, but this is no reason to adopt a casual attitude to their engagement or training. You will probably have many people approach you for a job whom you may well have the advantage of knowing already as customers. As it is unlikely that a vacancy will be available just when they want it, you then have the opportunity of observing them and getting to know them better. It may also be a simple matter to obtain the opinions of their friends and acquaintances in casual conversation. Thus, when the occasion arises, you may well have one or two candidates for a vacancy

115

Running Your Own Pub

already 'vetted' and ready to step into the job.

Taking on complete strangers is another matter. It is important to be as certain as possible that an applicant is entirely suitable. Much can be gleaned at an interview, not only from the answers to your questions, but also from behaviour and appearance. A person who is to care about your customers will also show consideration to you and due regard to the occasion in such matters as punctuality, politeness, good humour, friendliness and a reasonable standard of dress.

It should go without saying that your attitude should be the same. Do not paint an untrue picture of the job. Explain exactly what the duties and the rate of pay are to be. Make clear what you expect in the way of conscientiousness, behaviour to the public, standards of dress, honesty, hygiene and so on. Do not make promises which you may not be able to fulfil.

References should always be obtained and taken up. A telephone call is often all that is necessary, and although people generally lean on the lenient side towards ex-employees, it soon becomes obvious if you have a doubtful one. A most useful question is, 'Would you re-engage them?'

There is nothing to stop you employing people on a trial basis, as long as this is clearly understood and that a time limit is set. It should only take a few sessions to weed out the bad ones.

The law requires that you do not discriminate on grounds of race or sex where more than five people are employed. It is also a matter of law that when you engage someone a contract of employment comes into existence, even if it is only verbal. I would heartily recommend a written contract. It does not have to be a complicated document as long as it clearly states the terms and conditions of employment. This saves any possible misunderstanding, and could make all the difference should an industrial tribunal case arise. In any case, you must provide a written statement of these terms and conditions within 13 weeks to any employee who works more than 16 hours a week. The statement must specify:

116

The names of the employer and employee.
The job title.
The date employment began.
The scale and intervals of pay.
The hours of work.
Holidays and holiday pay.
Sickness and injury payments and notification requirements.
Amount of notice on termination of employment by both parties.
The procedure regarding employee grievances.
Disciplinary rules.

Those people who work more than eight but less than 16 hours per week must be given such a statement within five years.

Your nearest Jobcentre or Social Security office is able to help if you need advice or information about the employment of staff.

Training

Good staff always respond well to good training. People need to know how you like things done, and are not at their best when uncertain. It is a good idea to start right away on a formal training session. This helps to dispel any false impression the trainee may have gained, as a result of your professionally relaxed manner, that your organisation is not business-like and disciplined.

Go right back to basics. Explain your business philosophy so that they understand what lies behind the way in which you wish your customers to be treated. Make sure that they appreciate what a pub is all about, and why people go to it. This should then lead on to an explanation of the attitude which naturally springs from this philosophy, and which you expect them to have towards their job.

It then becomes obvious that the day-to-day details, such as the right glass, the correct method of dispense, cleanliness and attentiveness to the customers' needs, must all be carried out exactly according to your instructions.

Running Your Own Pub

The more important of these can be written down, not only to ensure that there are no misunderstandings or mistakes, but also to give your staff the security of having the information to hand, without the necessity of asking.

I always used to tell my staff that there is never any time in a pub when there is 'nothing to do'. This helps to keep them alert to the need to clean ashtrays, clear tables, clean shelves and the counter top, wash up and watch for empty glasses.

Training should never really stop. Keep an eye out for mistakes, and for any relaxation of professional attitudes. Every time they act without total proficiency they risk losing a customer whose potential spending power over the years may be enormous. Make them aware of this fact, and remind them every so often of your basic policy.

As the instructor, of course, you must remember that you are the example. Your own standards should at all times be the highest.

Supervision

It is easy to become over-anxious about your employees' honesty and ability. Constant heavy-handed supervision will only cause resentment, and such a mood will bring about the opposite of that which you intend.

If you do have good grounds for mistrusting anybody, then have it out with them and, if necessary, get rid of them (see pages 120-21). Otherwise be observant, and let the correction of mistakes become a part of your positive training schedule rather than an occasion for recrimination. Nobody can be expected to do the job perfectly from day one. Make it plain that your concern is to improve their performance not to hand out blame.

It is far more important to be generous with praise and thanks. There is no reason why you should not say 'thank you' at the end of every session. Even warmer sentiments, and perhaps a bonus or a free drink, should be offered after a particularly busy time such as Christmas and New Year.

118

Staff

People with a good training background, reinforced with the knowledge that their efforts are appreciated, come to see themselves as important parts of the whole enterprise. The success of the business becomes a measure of their own success, and so they are motivated to try harder for the good of the whole.

This feeling of mutual interest can be further encouraged by letting them in on the hard facts of your business. Many people are wary of divulging information, but if you want staff to cooperate and feel a part of the organisation, why not let them know something about the degree to which their efforts are helping? You do not have to give a falsely rosy picture. The information that this year you have managed to cut down your overdraft by 50 per cent shows not only that, with their help, business is improving, but also one of the hard facts about the risks and stresses that you, as the boss, must bear.

Be receptive also to their problems and questions. Encourage suggestions about how customer service or working conditions might be improved. This shows enthusiasm, and it is surprising what a fresh outlook can come up with.

Staff drinks, whether paid for by you or by customers, should be subject to strict rules: only the most moderate drinking should be allowed during working hours. After closing time is the occasion for relaxing over any drinks bought for them.

It is good practice to make it clear in the terms and conditions of employment what your rules are, especially regarding the acceptance of drinks and the handling of money. This not only helps to prevent misunderstandings, but also leaves everyone in no doubt at the outset about what you expect from them. Furthermore, such precautions could be invaluable in any industrial tribunal proceedings.

Delegation

Although you will need to make sure that your ideas predominate in the running of the pub, and although it is your personality that will primarily influence the atmosphere, you will find that in time certain of your staff will build up a following of their own. As long as such custom is not totally at odds with the general ambience, this can only be to your advantage. Indeed, the fact that they have by their enthusiasm and positive attitude attracted a clientele in their own right merely justifies your faith in them.

Sooner or later you will need people whom you can trust, not only with your till, but also with your clientele and your business as a whole. Your time off is of paramount importance, and it is therefore essential to encourage those staff who you feel can step into your shoes when necessary. It is a mistake to suppose that you are totally indispensable.

Dismissal

Dismissing a member of staff is nowadays a very tricky business. Legislation is weighted in favour of the employee, and an industrial tribunal can be an expensive business for the employer.

Instant dismissal is possible for gross misconduct. However, such misconduct would have to be proved should the matter come before a tribunal, and this may turn out to be very difficult. Normally a person working 16 hours or more a week is entitled to one week's notice after one month of continuous employment, and two weeks' notice after two years. Thereafter one week's notice must be given for each year of employment up to 12 weeks. A person working eight to 16 hours per week is entitled to the same notice after five years of employment.

In a case of misconduct or inefficiency an oral warning should be given first, after the employee has had the opportunity to put his case. Where possible it is advisable to have a witness to these proceedings, and a written record should be kept of the date and nature of the offence, and of the action taken.

A final warning should be given in writing, allowing the employee to put his case, once again with a witness present. The warning should tell him the nature of the offence, remind him of previous oral warnings with dates, make it clear that dismissal will

Staff

follow further lapses, and advise him of the grievance procedure.

Before dismissal it is wise to be sure that no alternative action is possible. For example, in the case of inefficiency it may be that he can be employed in another capacity. It is also essential that you have proof of the misconduct or inefficiency, with reliable witnesses, and written records of any interviews or warnings on the matter. Dismissal should be confirmed in writing and should remind him of your warnings and the dates, advise him of the reasons for dismissal, remind him of the grievance procedure mentioned in the written warning, and state the notice entitlement laid out in his contract of employment with the date when his employment ends. You may give pay in lieu of notice if the employee agrees.

This procedure should be followed even if the person concerned has not reported for work for some time. Unless he has clearly resigned it should never be assumed that he has terminated his own employment, as a tribunal almost certainly will not.

All told, great caution must be exercised in these matters. If you are in any doubt seek advice. Useful publications are available from ACAS and the DHSS.

Chapter 9
Pub-keeping and the Law

Licensing law is tremendously complex and a constant cause of debate and difficulty within and without the trade. The publican, although he is expected to, cannot possibly know more than a fraction of the law applicable to him and his business. However, he is one of the few people outside the police force who has a duty to enforce the law on his premises. Furthermore, infringement of the law can bring about not only straightforward financial penalties, but also the loss of his licence, and of his source of income. He must therefore be prepared to take his responsibilities seriously, can in no circumstances afford to risk the rigour of the law, and must at all times cooperate to the full with those whose duty it is to enforce it.

Police

It must be remembered, however, that the legal system is designed not so much to punish, as to protect the citizens of this country. Cooperation with the police and magistrates can also ensure the protection of your right to carry on and enjoy your business peacefully. In the licensed trade, should you be unfortunate enough to need the assistance of the police, and you almost certainly will at some time in your career, you will be more than grateful for their prompt and efficient response to your call. There is, from your point of view, no advantage in breaking the law. On the other hand, it can be a great comfort to know that its officers are on your side.

I well remember the evening in my early days when about a dozen young men whom I had banned for various forms of misbehaviour of a violent nature,

Pub-keeping and the Law

turned up en masse expecting the mere threat of their numbers to persuade me to serve them. I refused, but frankly I was grateful that the bar counter hid my quaking knees. On their point-blank refusal to leave I called the police. Two officers swiftly arrived and with the utmost courtesy suggested to the 'gentlemen' that they might like to move on, which they did without more ado. The whole operation was carried out so quietly, efficiently and discreetly that I believe none of my more respectable customers, mostly peacefully dining, even realised what had happened.

Set up friendly relations with the local force right from the start (not forgetting that the entertainment of a police officer on duty on your premises is a serious offence). Even before taking over a pub introduce yourself at the station, and enquire about any particular matters relevant to the licensed trade in the area, such as persons known to be habitual troublemakers, or more serious than usual under-age drinking problems. Ask how they can help in times of difficulty and what is the quickest way to contact them at any hour. Seek their advice about the security of your premises, the car parking arrangements, and vehicle access. Show, in other words, your willingness to cooperate in matters of mutual concern. Once you have made it plain that you are a responsible landlord, concerned with keeping a respectable and orderly house, many of the worries which concern publicans will be reduced. Not least, your requests for extensions of hours, occasional licences, supper licences, and alterations to the premises will be viewed in a more favourable light.

Licence

The sheer volume of licensing law makes it wholly impracticable for me to do more than give some indication of those matters which you are most likely to come across in the day-to-day running of your pub.

On change-over day the magistrates will grant a protection order which allows you to carry on the business until the next transfer sessions when you will once again have to attend court to be granted the

123

full on-licence. From that time you must display a notice in a conspicuous place, most often over the front door, with your name and the items which you are licensed to sell. The licence has to be renewed every year at the Annual Licensing Meeting which must be held in the first fortnight in February. The local clerk to the licensing justices will advise you of the date. You may attend, and in some areas may be required to do so. The renewal can be opposed, especially if the police feel that, by constantly breaking the law for example, you have shown yourself to be unfit to run a public house. In this case you will be notified beforehand and will have to be there. Otherwise it is usually a straightforward matter, your main duty being the payment of the fee.

Permitted hours

Your licence enables you to sell liquor to be consumed on the premises only during permitted hours. Within certain limits these may vary in different areas, and it is necessary to enquire about them from the clerk to the licensing justices. Ten minutes' drinking-up time is allowed at the end of each session. Sales for consumption off the premises are covered by the same restrictions unless the justices have allowed a specific area, with no internal communication to the parts of the premises where on-licence sales take place, to enjoy the permitted hours for off-licences.

After-hours drinking is sometimes looked upon by certain members of the general public as fair game. The customer himself risks a heavy fine for his simple pleasures. The landlord's penalty can be even higher as he will be fined for each and every customer involved. Also, the establishment that gains a reputation for 'a late drink', (and that reputation will sooner or later reach the ears of the police) soon finds itself entertaining all those who have spent the rest of the evening, and most of their money, drinking elsewhere. Such customers have a habit of taking a considerable time over just one final drink, and the landlord's returns for the risk he has taken, the fuel he has wasted and the sleep he has missed, are minimal and by no means sufficient justification.

Right from the start refuse all requests for 'just one more' after time. They will soon get the message, and leave you to concentrate on the job of making real profits within legal hours.

Entertainment of friends and employees

Bona fide friends or employees can be entertained by the licensee in any part of the house, at any hour, provided it is at his own expense. Customers cannot, however, suddenly become friends at closing time in an attempt to get round the law. It is wise to let the police know of your plans for any such event.

Residents

Residents may purchase intoxicating liquor at any time.

Extension of hours

Extensions are not necessarily the great money-making spree they are generally thought to be. Unless you are sure of a pub full of free-spending drinkers at the normal closing hour, then the fee payable, the extra staff wages, the fuel and light expenses, and the additional work may well wipe out any extra profit. Except at obviously profitable times such as New Year's Eve or the local football team's victory celebrations (and I have known even those to be a damp squib), the pros and cons must be very carefully weighed up. When the extension has been asked for by customers, it may well be advisable to ask them to pay the court fee and even the extra wages. If the night does go well you can always make a generous refund afterwards.

Extensions may be sought only for 'special occasions', and you may find that the magistrates have different ideas from yourself about what constitutes them. They will not consider any function organised by yourself for your own profit a special occasion, and are nowadays tending to dismiss regularly recurring celebrations such as ordinary birthdays.

It is common for extensions for the public holidays of the year to be granted *en bloc*, sometimes for the payment of only one fee. This may be organised by

Running Your Own Pub

the local Licensed Victuallers' Association for its members, or a brewery for its tenants, otherwise you must apply yourself. It is certainly a good idea to get all the extensions for the year for known occasions, such as Christmas and other bank holidays, arranged at one time. The clerk to the licensing justices will let you have the necessary forms and advise on the procedure in your area. Generally, good notice is required, and it is always necessary to inform the police who will be asked in court if they have any objections or comment to make. If sufficient notice is given it is, in some areas, not necessary to attend the hearing, but it may pay to be on hand in case the bench needs assurance on any point, and it does no harm to be recognised as a cooperative and helpful licensee.

Occasional licences
Occasional licences are temporary ones granted to cover a function taking place outside the licensed premises, such as a dance in the village hall. Once again, these events are often not great money spinners. The numbers expected to attend by optimistic organisers are very rarely attained, and it is safe to assume that a fair proportion will be non-drinkers. There is a lot of extra work involved, as well as the expense of transport and extra staff, the cost of hire of equipment and the difficulty of gauging what, and how much, drink to order. Of course they *can* be highly profitable and give you the advantage of an income from two establishments at the same time. If you do intend to cater for such events then it is well worth getting properly organised, with suitable transport and equipment, and staff you can rely on to help with the heavy work as well as serve. Then make the most of it by letting local organisations know, by letter if necessary, that you have the facilities to provide a bar at their functions. It is usually the practice nowadays to charge for the licence, and sometimes to ask them to cover costs such as staff and transport. You could offer to refund these on a pro rata basis according to the takings at the end of the evening.

The premises on which the function is held are, for the duration of the licence, licensed premises under your control. Only you, as the licensee, can sell liquor on those premises, and your responsibilities are the same as in your pub. In other words, it is *your* duty, not the organisers', to ensure that the proceedings are orderly and that drunkenness, gaming, the serving of minors with alcohol, or after-hours drinking do not take place.

Supper licence

A supper hour certificate allows you to serve alcohol for one hour after the normal evening closing time, only for consumption with a meal served at the same time, and in a part of the premises normally set apart for the service of table meals. This can be a mixed blessing. It is hard to convince your drinking customers that they must drink up and go home if they are aware that others are still merrily indulging. You often find yourself hanging around for another hour while a besotted couple gaze into each others' eyes over the remains of a last drink bought hours before. On the other hand, it can be exasperating to have to refuse further service to a party still well into the swing of the evening, just at the point where they are in the mood for highly profitable after-dinner drinks. My overall feeling is that your basic policy comes into play again, and this is another way in which you can cater for your customers' enjoyment.

Application is made to the clerk to the justices for a hearing by the magistrates at a licensing session, and the police must be notified. Your premises may well be inspected to ensure that there is in fact an area normally set apart for the service of table meals.

Entertainment licence

Your pub licence allows you to stage entertainment on your premises provided that no more than two performers are involved. Spontaneous singing or dancing by your customers is also covered. Organised entertainment on any greater scale requires an entertainment licence from the local district council. You will have to provide safety precautions such as emergency exits and lighting, and adequate fire-fighting facilities. The number of people allowed to attend will

127

be limited according to the size of the premises. Possible nuisance to nearby residents and the views of the police will be taken into consideration. The licence has to be renewed annually, and complaints from residents or police may well lead to a refusal of renewal.

The expense will almost certainly be considerable, but once the facilities are there they can be a most useful source of income.

Special hours certificate and extended hours order
A special hours certificate can be granted up to 2 am on premises where an entertainment licence is in force and where the relevant part is structurally adapted, and is actually to be used, for music and dancing and substantial refreshment. An extended hours order is similar, but cannot be granted beyond 1 am. Both are applied for through the clerk to the licensing justices. Obviously, such facilities are highly desirable to the holder of an entertainment licence.

Alterations

When making alterations to licensed premises the consent of the licensing justices must be sought. Plans are usually required, and the premises will probably be inspected. Customer convenience and safety, adequate serving facilities, sufficient exits and the unobstructed view from behind the counter of all areas, are some of the matters which may be considered. It is wise to consult the clerk to the justices, the police and the fire officer before drawing up your plans.

Children

No person under 14 years of age is allowed on licensed premises except the children of the licensee, anyone who is resident, or anyone who passes through on their way from one part of the building to another. A person over 16 but under 18 cannot be sold intoxicating liquor, is not allowed to consume it on licensed premises, and must not have it bought for them by someone else. The only exception is where that person consumes beer, porter, cider or perry with a meal in an area which is set apart for the service of meals. No person under the age of 18 can be employed in a bar when it is open for the sale and consumption of intoxicating liquor.

It is illegal to sell cigarettes or tobacco to anyone under 16.

Police and magistrates are particularly concerned about under-age drinking. If you have any doubts at all about the age of a customer, refuse to serve them. Do not accept documentary evidence of their age unless you are certain that the document applies to the person concerned. Make sure that your staff understand their duty in this respect.

Drunkenness

You must not permit drunkenness or any violent or quarrelsome behaviour on your premises. You can expel anybody guilty of such behaviour, and a police officer is obliged to assist you if requested. Refusal to quit licensed premises by such a person upon being requested to do so is a statutory offence.

In practice I have found that force in these matters tends to inflame the situation, and leads to violence, foul language, damage, injury or at the very least embarrassment and discomfort to your other customers who may be sufficiently disturbed to take their custom elsewhere. If a civil but firm request to leave does not work, then the mere presence, or even the threat of the presence, of a police officer will almost certainly have the desired effect.

Betting, gaming and lotteries

Betting and the passing of betting slips are not allowed. Gaming or the playing of a game of chance for money or money's-worth is prohibited except for dominoes and cribbage. Games of skill such as darts, billiards and skittles are permitted.

Small lotteries, not for private gain, may be held

when incidental to an entertainment such as a dance. The tickets may only be sold at the time, and there must be no cash prizes. Lotteries promoted by a registered charitable society, not for private gain, are also permissible.

Amusement machines

A licence must be obtained from the licensing justices for fruit machines, although this may be taken care of for you by your supplier. The fee is considerable. There is a limit on the amount which càn be charged for each chance to win, and on the amount which can be won on a machine on licensed premises.

Race relations and sex discrimination

It is unlawful to discriminate against a person on racial or sexual grounds. This applies to employees and job applicants as well as customers. It does not negate the publican's duty to keep an orderly house, or his right to refuse service on grounds other than race or sex.

Liquid measures

Draught beer and cider must be sold in quantities of one-third, one-half or multiples of one-half pint, and must be served in a stamped glass of equivalent capacity except where they are dispensed by stamped measuring equipment in sight of the customer.

Whisky, gin, rum and vodka can only be sold in quantities of one-fourth, one-fifth or one-sixth of a gill, or multiples of those quantities, except in the case of mixed drinks containing three or more liquids. You must display a notice saying in which of these quantities these spirits are supplied.

Wine in carafes can only be sold in quantities of one-half, three-quarters or one litre, or 10 or 20 fluid ounces. A notice must be displayed showing what quantities are sold.

A Trading Standards Officer will call upon you regularly and check all the stamped or sealed measures, including optics, on your premises. He will also ensure that your pint and half-pint draught beer glasses are government stamped, and check for dilution or adulteration. He will want to see that you are displaying the notices regarding quantities sold mentioned above, and price-lists for the items of food and drink you are selling. If there is a separate restaurant or dining area a price-list must be displayed at or near both the interior and the street entrances. The prices shown must include VAT.

Dilution and adulteration

All wines, beers and spirits should be sold as they are received. The addition of water or any other liquid, including a weaker with a stronger beer, or a lower grade wine or spirit with a higher grade one, even if they are of the same alcoholic strength, is a very serious offence.

Copyright

If you have a radio, television, any system for transmitting music or any live performance of music in your pub you become liable for royalties, payable to the composers. This is organised by The Performing Rights Society, 29-33 Berners Street, London W1A 4PP, who will issue an annual licence, the fee for which is based on what equipment you have and to what extent music is performed.

Credit

It is illegal to give credit for drinks consumed on the premises and such debts cannot be legally recovered. If you give credit, or get into the habit of cashing cheques, you will quickly find that more and more people will want to avail themselves of your generosity. Quite apart from the question of the law, the headaches and frustrations of trying to recover money owed, or chasing up bounced cheques, far outweigh considerations of good customer relations.

Chapter 10
Daily Operation of the Pub

Running a pub is not just a job but a whole way of life. What is more, it is a way of life completely different from anything you have been used to. Weekends, formerly days of rest and relaxation, will now be your busiest working days. You will be on duty most evenings after already having put in the best part of a full day's work. Leisure-time activities, including TV watching or even visiting a pub, will almost disappear. The whole rhythm of your life will change.

Daily organisation

It is not a good idea to attempt to hang on to the patterns, developed over a lifetime and shared by most people, of your old way of living. Think about your *new* work schedule and reorganise your day around it. For example, I unthinkingly maintained the idea of three meals a day, taken as near as possible to the times I had been used to: I breakfasted when I got up, had lunch at about 3 o'clock, just after closing time, and dinner at about 11.30 at night. This meant that during the whole of lunch-time, and from about 8 o'clock in the evening, instead of being a relaxed and easy-going host, I was ravenously hungry and consequently extremely irritable. Furthermore, I went to bed weighed down by a heavy meal which spelt ruin for my digestion and my waistline.

Having belatedly woken up to the fact that meal-times are not sacrosanct, I reorganised myself. I had something very light on rising, an apple or a slice of toast. Just before opening time I ate a substantial breakfast, or brunch, which carried me through the lunch-time session, and then had the main meal of the

132

Daily Operation of the Pub

day at about 5 o'clock. Thus fortified I could tackle the evening's work, and finish off with a light snack, if necessary, at night.

Think about the jobs you have to get through during the course of the day, and organise yourself to carry them out in the most efficient way and with the minimum wear and tear on yourself. You must not forget that your primary duty is to be the genial host, not a work-weary slouch who can't wait for your customers to go home so that you can put your feet up.

Paperwork

As you will not be going to bed before midnight, I would recommend rising no earlier than 8 am unless you are one of those who can manage with very little sleep. I then used to tackle the paperwork while my mind was still reasonably fresh and in working order. First do the cashing up, entering the results in the account book and putting the day's float in the till, which should be locked until opening time. The mail can then be dealt with and any invoices entered in the invoice register. The cash book should be brought up to date, and any surplus money prepared for banking. If any orders are due, then go through your stock cards and prepare them. Make sure all of the day's paperwork is cleared up.

Cleaning

You will almost certainly find it well worth your while to employ a cleaner eventually, but it is a good idea to do it yourself for a while so that you know what and how things should be done, and about how long they take.

Any open fires should be dealt with first, ash removed and new supplies of fuel brought in. All rooms should be dusted and ashtrays emptied. Keep a 1½-in paint brush and a separate cloth for this job. The tables, chairs, bar counter and back shelves need thorough washing and polishing, and fresh beer mats and bar towels put out. Floors should be cleaned as appropriate. After a particularly heavy night the

133

carpets can be brushed with a stiff broom before vacuum cleaning to remove cigarette stubs and packets, crisp bags, spent matches and other larger items of rubbish.

The ladies' toilet is one of the most important rooms in the place. It must be thoroughly cleaned every day and soap, clean towels and toilet paper put out. There should be a spare roll in each cubicle. It will occasionally be stolen but pilfering is one of those things publicans must learn to live with, I'm afraid. Better to lose a toilet roll than to lose your customers' goodwill. A vase of flowers is a nice touch here, and a chair, plenty of mirrors, coathangers, and a surface for handbags and make-up are essential.

The gents' toilet need not necessarily be quite so well furnished, but there is no reason why it should be an unpleasant place to visit. Smell is the big enemy, but thorough cleansing with disinfectant at least once a day should eliminate this. I found a small mop soaked with undiluted bleach particularly effective for urinals. If you use channel blocks make sure that the smell does not spread beyond the toilets and percolate around the bars. It is a common fault, and that disinfectant smell destroys a pub atmosphere.

Do not overlook the outside of the pub. The front doorstep, paths and patios should all be swept. The car park and beer garden should be checked for rubbish, and the outside tables and chairs washed and ashtrays emptied. In the summer, sun umbrellas should be put out as soon as possible, as they are a part of the attractive picture your pub should present, even outside opening hours.

Each day some time should be spent on one of the weekly jobs, such as cleaning windows, polishing brass and copper, and cleaning pictures and *bric-à-brac*. Carpets should be shampooed, and walls and ceilings washed at least twice a year. Machines can be hired for the carpets, but there are firms which specialise in the big tasks, including a really thorough job of the kitchen. You may find it well worth paying their charges to relieve yourself of the arduous work involved. The day-to-day cleaning of the kitchens should be carried out as you go along, finishing off each session with a thorough wipe down and mop.

Bottling up

The previous day's empty bottles must be removed, sorted and put in their correct empty crates. Take a note of the numbers of each type of full bottle required and fetch them from the bottle store, making sure that the oldest stock is taken first. If any distance is involved use a sack-truck or trolley.

Remove any bottles remaining on the back shelves. Wipe the shelves and the new bottles before putting them up. Replace the remaining bottles at the front to ensure stock rotation.

Bottles on optic should be checked and replaced where necessary, and stocks of crisps, nuts, cigarettes and tobacco replenished. Fill the ice buckets with fresh ice. Wash and refill the water jugs. If they are stained with lime soak them in a vinegar solution overnight.

Make sure that there are sufficient lemons, cherries and other garnishes, as well as straws and cocktail sticks. Check soda siphons, lime juice dispensers, orange squash and lemonade bottles. Replenish the cold shelf and refrigerator. Clean out the containers for empties and the rubbish bins. Replace soiled glass cloths. Empty bottle-top containers.

Cellar work

If the pipes are due for cleaning get that under way first. Remove all the empty barrels, sealing those that need it. Carry out any necessary preparation on the cask conditioned beers as outlined in Chapter 5. Make sure that full follow-up canisters of keg beer are to hand.

Scrub and hose down the floor and walls, paying particular attention to areas around any casks that are working. Check that you have CO_2 gas pressure, and that a spare cylinder is near at hand. If any deliveries are due, get all empties counted and ready for collection. If you are cleaning the pipes make sure

Running Your Own Pub

you have flushed them through and that good, clear beer is flowing.

I once opened up forgetting that I still had cleaning fluid throughout the system. As always happens when you are ill-prepared, the army chose to do exercises in the area on that particular day. As soon as I opened the door in poured a crowd of thirsty soldiers. When I started to pull the first pint I realised my predicament. The soldiers were in no mood to be patient as, panic-stricken, I pulled through the fluid and flushed out the pipes. It was a good 10 minutes before I could start serving good beer. I was grateful that they had left their weapons outside!

Food preparation

Ninety per cent of the midday demand for food comes between 1 o'clock and quarter past, and customers with short lunch-times do not like to be kept waiting. Anything you can do to be ready for the rush is invaluable. Certainly make sure that crockery, cutlery, napkins and trays are all to hand. Garnishes can be prepared beforehand and placed conveniently for use in a hurry. To some extent cold meals can be made ready; take care not to cause drying out, melting or curling edges. Bottle-necks at the microwave oven can be partly alleviated by keeping popular dishes and soups hot on the stove, but never sacrifice quality to convenience. Within reasonable bounds it is better to have a customer wait for good food than serve rubbish quickly.

Odds and ends

Banking, buying change and shopping may need to be done. Chalk-written menus and notices may have to be changed, and all signs put out or checked for position. Fires must be lit or heating turned on, flowers changed and plants watered, coffee machines filled. The draught beers should all be tasted and opened wines checked.

Brunch

This is the point where I would take a shower and sit down to a substantial and well-earned meal. In practice I soon found that I just could not do all the above jobs in the time available. I usually had a cleaner and a cellarman/bottler-up as well as kitchen staff. Paperwork, shopping, banking and supervision of everyone else took all my time. You will very quickly sort out your own organisation.

Opening time

The pub should be in full operation before the first customer walks in the door. A warm, welcoming bar and a cheery greeting will persuade him that this is a place to come back to. Any custom you can get during the quieter times should be encouraged, in the hope of making them busier times. Do not be tempted to leave the heating turned down or the lights turned off just because few people are around, and do not put off getting the ice ready or the lemons to hand. You must be fully ready to serve just as soon as you open the doors.

If you are quiet, then this is the time to check and clean the optics, wipe the back shelves and the bottles on them, polish up the beer pumps, replace dud light bulbs, clean and refill pickle and condiment containers. Never leave the bar unattended, however, both for obvious security reasons, and to ensure that any customer receives a proper welcome.

Closing time

Let your customers down gently at the end of the session. Try to avoid giving them the feeling that you are rushing them out as this can completely nullify your efforts to give an impression of warm hospitality. Everybody is aware of the licensing laws, and very few will need really pointed reminders. Call last orders at least 10 minutes before time to get everyone used to the idea. At the last bell turn off the lights in the beer pumps and any outside ones. At the end of drinking-up time extinguish those over the bar and any in the windows. By now people should not be drinking, but there is nothing in law to say that they have to be off the premises. Give them a chance to collect themselves together and make visits to the toilet, before switching off main lights, clearing up the last glasses, and generally making it clear that it is time to go.

After everyone has gone, lock all doors and check that the windows are securely closed, particularly those in the toilets. This is a favourite point of illegal entry, and it has been known for a thief to hide in the toilet after using the lunch-time session to give the place a look over. Once the coast is clear it is a simple matter to help himself and slip out of the front door.

Empty the till at least of notes and put them in the safe. It may be necessary to top up the bottle shelves, and a quick check should be made in the cellar. Tables and the counter will need wiping, and beer mats replaced or renewed. The floor may require a quick clean, and make sure that the toilet paper situation is all right.

Empty the ashtrays into a metal bucket which should be taken, with all the other rubbish, straight out to a metal dustbin situated well away from the building to minimise the risk of fire. The bars should be left completely ready for the evening session.

The same rule applies to the kitchen. All food should be put away, and everything should be spotlessly clean. Check that all appliances are turned off.

There will inevitably be some chore to catch up on, but try to make a point of getting some rest during the afternoon, followed by a substantial, relaxed meal.

Evening session

The same procedure should be followed as at lunchtime. If it is dark do not forget the car park and other outside lights. Make sure that they are all working.

At closing time it is even more important to be security conscious than in the afternoon. After everyone has gone, check the whole premises, including all outside areas, for anyone hanging around. I once found a lady fast asleep in the toilet!

Daily Operation of the Pub

Beer spillages congeal overnight, so wipe off the tables, bar counter and back shelves, and wash the drip trays. Put the beer to bed making sure that all spiles (pegs) are in place, and that the CO_2 gas is turned off. Empty the ashtrays and take out the rubbish.

At this point I used to collapse and unwind with a large scotch and a small sandwich. I resisted watching television or video films as this invariably meant that it was 2 or 3 o'clock before I got to bed. With another busy day coming up tomorrow, you need all the sleep you can get.

Chapter 11
Time Off

The last chapter will have given you some idea of the work load you will be facing. What is more this will go on day after day. Neither mind nor body can withstand prolonged physical work and mental pressures such as this. Without rest and a chance to get away from the business atmosphere once in a while, the strain begins to tell. Minor illnesses tend to appear. You become forgetful and devoid of creative ideas. Irritability creeps in. Worries assume exaggerated proportions.

In normal circumstances, if you wanted to punish yourself in this way then it would be your affair. However, you now have responsibilities to your customers, your staff and to your business, and it is your duty to ensure that you are fully capable of discharging them.

It is obvious that a weary, irritable and ailing landlord is quite unable to generate the genial atmosphere that is your greatest selling point. Things will start to be too much trouble. Staff relations will suffer. Customers will become matters of inconvenience. Standards will slide disastrously and your basic policy will fly out of the window.

If you get up at 8 o'clock, manage two hours off in the afternoon, and retire at midnight, you are on the go for 14 hours a day. After a six-day week you have worked twice as long as most people do. Time off is essential. You will find that your regulars will be amazed. 'What, more time off?' will be the comment when you have finally managed to get away at midday on your day off for a few precious hours, after having done two weeks' work for their one. Do not let this stop you. It is true that people come to your pub because they like *you*, and want to see you behind the

140

bar. They will be disappointed if you are not there, and may even go elsewhere on your day off. But their loyalty has only been brought about by your friendliness and hospitality. If you are too exhausted to maintain it, then they won't come at all.

Staff

Of course, staff will be your main worry, but if you have trained them well, there is no reason why they should not manage without you. You must have confidence in them, and must not assume that in your absence everything will fall apart. A pub becomes a personal thing, your 'baby', but even babies can be trusted to a sitter now and then. There is little point in having time off if you take your worries with you and keep wondering what is going on back home.

Many of your fears, and any uncertainties the staff may have, can be allayed by leaving strict, written instructions. Security must, of course, be a primary consideration. Proper arrangements must be made regarding locking up and the safe keeping of cash.

Which day?

If you take the quietest day off, then it is the day when you will be least missed. At the same time, perhaps that day, being an area where your business could stand improvement, is when you should be actively trying to win more custom. I took Sunday night off for years under the impression that it was definitely a dead duck. However, on a recent visit to my old pub I discovered that the new landlord had built up a very healthy Sunday evening eating trade.

In most areas Monday certainly seems to be a day that will not come alive, whatever you do, and it is therefore a favourite day off for publicans. On the other hand, I had a young couple take over for me on Mondays on a regular basis, and such was their popularity that they built up a very useful following of their own, and I had to admit that they seemed to do better than I could have done.

In any case, you will have to accept the possibility

of some loss of trade because of your absence, and regard it as a part of the price you have to pay for your leisure. It is certainly better than risking the loss of all of it because tiredness brings about a deterioration in your professionalism.

Getting away

It is essential to get right away. While you are there staff will have queries, customers will want to see you, the telephone will keep on ringing and you will notice all those little things that need doing. Leave as early as possible, stay away all day, and resist the temptation to telephone to see if everything is all right. If there are any problems you will be better fitted to face them after a day's uninterrupted break.

It seems to be almost traditional that landlords spend their time off in other people's pubs. This has its advantages. It is not a bad idea to see how others do things—I have pinched many good ideas from other publicans. It is also pleasant to talk shop with someone else in the trade occasionally. However, it can easily lead to your leisure time being spent in a haze of alcohol, which is not particularly healthy and, I suspect, not really relaxing.

There is no reason why you should lose touch with whatever leisure pursuits you followed before entering the trade. Golf, squash, walking and other such physical activities are excellent. Fishing is a little more gentle, but perhaps even more relaxing and away from it all. Visit friends or relations or go to the cinema or theatre, and don't get back till late in the evening or you are bound to get lured into the bar.

Holidays

Take a good holiday every year. You will have earned it. There are reputable agencies who can supply experienced and trustworthy people to run the pub while you are away. You will find their advertisements in the trade press, or your brewery may well be able to recommend someone. It is quite expensive and makes the total cost of the holiday rather high.

However, you will come back refreshed, re-charged, and full of enthusiasm and good ideas to improve your business.

I am not at all sure that the traditional landlord's holiday—two weeks' hard boozing and living it up in an expensive hotel in Tenerife—is necessarily a good idea. I remember two sets of publican friends of mine going off together for such a spree. They came back looking much more exhausted than when they left. Both blamed the other couple for forcing the pace too much. Complete relaxation is the answer, either of the 'do absolutely nothing but lie on the beach' category, or physically active 'get away from it all' variety.

Personal life

Guard your personal life. If you are single, friends will find it hard to understand why you have so little time to devote to them, and will be bewildered by your unusual hours and life-style. Make the most of your time off to cement good relations. Loyal friends away from the business are invaluable.

Married couples will be sharing the load, but will see very little of each other in conditions free of work-day stress. Extreme patience and understanding are necessary, and getting away together particularly important, as long as you do not take your work with you.

The trade is notoriously hard on marriages. You will have to try extra hard if yours is to remain happy and stable. On the other hand, a partnership in a successful career as well as in a loving union does have the potential for a much more complete and satisfying relationship.

Children need special consideration. I am not at all sure that it is such a bad way of life for them as many people suggest. Certainly for older children, having to fend for themselves to some extent at least, while their parents are busy, helps to develop a sense of self-reliance and responsibility. When the family can get together the occasion becomes much more of a special one. A main meal at about 5 o'clock fits in well with school hours, and ensures one very definite time when the family is together each day. For the rest of the evening homework, television, friends and outside interests do not leave much time or appetite for parental company in any case.

I am convinced that my three daughters gained immeasurably from coming into contact with a much wider cross-section of the community than most children, and from observing at close quarters the world of adult relationships, work and business — the sort of education you don't get from books. What is more, a publican's daughter seems to have no problem finding boy friends!

Younger children need more time and attention, but sensible organisation and a greater use of staff should overcome the problem. I know of at least one couple with young children where the husband runs a very successful pub, while the wife follows almost entirely the traditional role of wife and mother, only appearing in the bar on a strictly social basis.

The thing that children need most from their parents is love and affection. On the occasions that you are together, show a real interest in them and their lives, and make your love for them clear.

Chapter 12
The Future

One of the greatest advantages, and the biggest challenge of being self-employed, is that your career and your future standard of living are almost entirely in your own hands. The overall economic situation will naturally make a difference, but even the effects of recession can be combated.

Of course, you may not wish to dramatically improve your lot. You may have found a business which provides sufficient income for your economic needs, as well as a fulfilling and satisfying career and way of life. Even so, in business you cannot afford to stand still: a static turnover is in fact, because of inflation, decreasing in value each year, while higher costs will be eating into your profits at an alarming rate. Furthermore, a fickle public will inevitably drift away from even the best pubs, unless constant efforts are made to attract new custom.

The moment you begin to feel complacent about your situation is a moment of danger. You must always be thinking ahead, seeking ways to increase the business, planning to improve next year's turnover and profits.

Strategy

Successful organisations develop a strategy for the future. They set targets, give themselves goals to aim for. Reaching the target is not actually so important as the stimulus they provide to urge one to do better.

Ask yourself how you see your situation in two, five, ten years' time. Comfortably ensconced in a small, friendly but popular pub, organised so as to minimise your work load and problems, or riding

145

Running Your Own Pub

around in an expensive car visiting each of your 10 highly successful establishments to collect the day's takings before flying off to your yacht in the Caribbean?

No, neither of these are just dreams. They are attainable by anybody. Successful people are those who have achieved their ambitions, however high, or however humble they may be. But first be absolutely sure that the dream is really what you want. If it is happiness you are seeking, are you sure that money will buy it? If it is peace and contentment, may not the reality be frustrating and less than fulfilling? Is the goal you seek worth the struggle to attain it?

Set yourself a target. For example, aim to pay off your overdraft within, say, 12 months, or your loan within five years. Promise yourself that you will have a larger establishment, a second pub, or have doubled your turnover by a particular date.

Make them realistic goals, and plan your approach to them in six-monthly steps, based on honest assessments of what you should be able to achieve by way of steadily increasing business. Now work out the methods by which you plan to bring about this increase over the next two six-monthly periods.

For example, you are presently taking on average £1000 per week, of which £150 is from food. The summer season is coming up and experience, or the previous landlord, has told you that the average figure will almost automatically go up to £1500 per week including £300 for food. You have a spare piece of land at the side of the pub, and an extra room that only seems to get used as a dumping ground. The land becomes a beer garden and the room a children's room. You spread the word, advertise and put out the appropriate signs, and you may well feel that you could double your food trade, that is £600 per week, and add another 50 per cent to your drinks business, making a total weekly turnover of £2400.

The following six months cover the quieter winter period, but there will be some spin-off from your spreading reputation for good food, and you have plans to open the old barn for discos at the weekends. Your projection may look like this:

146

The Future

	£
Average weekly take last winter	
Liquor	850
Food	150
Estimated increase	
Liquor 30%	255
Food 100%	150
Disco entrance fee £1.50, two nights with	
75 people per night	225
Estimated extra liquor sales, say £1	
per head	150
	1780

Against these figures must be set the extra expenses involved such as staff, electricity, advertising and the disc jockey's fees, as well as the cost of financing the scheme. Once again your cash flow chart will help you to gauge the feasibility of your plans and, once they are under way, to monitor their progress.

Such a strategy commits you to doing the necessary work to prepare the garden, the children's room and the disco barn; it gives you a target at which to aim; it provides a concrete framework for the realisation of your goals; and it concentrates the mind, so easily bogged down in routine matters, on the continual development of your enterprise. It also encourages you to keep alert to the signs of new directions in the trade as a whole, and to changes in the local markets that you are catering for. You will want to read the trade journals, attend trade exhibitions, and look critically at any pubs you visit, constantly seeking new ideas which you can use and develop. You will also keep abreast of local news and be aware of potential new markets, changing conditions, and increasing competition.

The whole of the first year in my first pub was spent simply running the place, from day to day. I had not given great consideration to how to increase trade, and had rather expected people to flock in just because the pub was there. I took a week's holiday during which I could not help noticing how much busier most pubs were than mine. This led me to try to work out why they were busier. I came back from that holiday not only refreshed but with my head bursting with ideas which I then put into practice. Within 12 months I had *quadrupled* my weekly takings.

Alternatives
Possibly the most potentially satisfying ambition for a publican is the steady growth of his conception of the perfect pub, playing its part within a particular community. Such a person will never make a fortune, but he can hope for a very comfortable living while also enjoying the very real rewards born out of his success in developing an organisation offering a high degree of service, enjoyment and satisfaction to the public. He will gradually create a network of friendships, business relationships, leisure interests and community activities more than sufficient to ensure a fulfilling life-style.

Those with different ambitions might aim to reach a monetary target in their present pub such as being able to finance the acquisition of larger or potentially more profitable premises. A few years' experience should have shown in which direction their interests and talents lie. A flair for catering could lead to the sort of establishment mainly devoted to food, with restaurants and function rooms as well as bar snack facilities. The hotel aspect could be explored. Country clubs, entertainment houses or simply a straightforward pub in a busier location could be considered. The possibilities are limitless.

This leads on to the idea of running more than one establishment. Once you have set the pattern in your first successful venture there is no reason why more or less the same formula should not work elsewhere. Your proven record will tend to smooth the path to further finance, and your experience will make the setting up of subsequent enterprises comparatively easy.

The opportunities are all there in the licensed trade. It is up to you to go out and grasp them.

Ideas for expansion

Let us have a look then at what can be done in your present establishment to increase business, assuming that you have already taken action in the fields previously discussed such as decor, signs, advertising and your own attitude.

The building

Take a close look at the existing building, the land around it and any outbuildings. Try to free your mind from any preconceptions which might limit your imagination. For example, many pubs have the landlord's private sitting-room on the ground floor. You may feel that this room is essential for your times of relaxation, but ignore that for a while and look for further ways it could be used for the benefit of the business. You can tackle the question of your private sitting-room later, perhaps by reorganising the upstairs living quarters.

Consider the storage spaces, utility rooms, even the kitchen. Could these be reorganised and put to better use as part of the public areas? In some cases, the private living quarters are far larger than necessary, and space could be given over to a small function or conference room. An outbuilding may stand conversion into a function hall, a children's room, a restaurant or an area for skittles, darts or other games. The grounds could be put to use as a beer garden, a car park, a caravan and camping park, or even for building motel units.

Before making any decision to act, however, two aspects must be taken into consideration. First the anticipated increased business must be sufficient to justify the capital expenditure involved, taking into account, if you own the premises, any likely effect on the overall value of the place.

Second, almost any alteration, to a greater or lesser extent, will change the character of the pub, especially where it is designed to provide facilities of a very different nature from those previously offered. There may be an adverse effect on the existing clientele, and possible consequent loss of trade from one part of the business must be more than adequately compensated for by any anticipated extra income.

Sports and events
There are also plenty of ways to generate interest and business within your existing set-up. For instance, have you developed the games in your pub to their fullest potential? Darts, skittles, dominoes, pool, cards and even shove ha'penny can all be exploited by organising house championships, inter-pub competitions and leagues, and visits by professional players. This can be extended to football, cricket, bowls or any other outside game, which in turn can lead to charity events, perhaps involving a showbiz team.

The local community might be prompted, with your help and support, to organise events such as carnivals, shows, exhibitions, fairs and rallies. Not only will these bring in extra business, but your active involvement will enhance your standing in the community, and generate favourable publicity for your establishment.

Special nights
Take full advantage of the special nights of the year, more especially those in quieter periods such as Burns' Night, St Valentine's Day, Guy Fawkes Night, Hallowe'en, your birthday, anniversaries and local celebrations as well as Christmas, New Year, Easter, May Day, Midsummer's Night and so on. Fancy dress parties are popular for these occasions, especially if there is a barbecue as well.

Happy hour makes any night special, especially if it applies to cocktails or the like. Not only can it bring in trade at times when things are normally quiet, but it is a fair bet that some of that trade will stay on for the rest of the evening.

Music
Regular music nights not only bring in more trade, but also help to give your pub the reputation as the place where all the fun is, where 'it all happens'. Ideally, you need a separate room so that a modest

entrance fee can be charged to help defray the performers' fees, otherwise you have to sell a lot of extra drinks to make the evening profitable. Do not forget also, that you may be turning away trade who do not happen to like the particular type of music on offer.

I have successfully used rock, country and western, folk, pop, jazz, string quartets, a real flamenco guitarist, comedians, even madrigal singers. Ask your customers to recommend performers. You may be surprised how much good music is available in your area, often at very reasonable rates. And why not hold your own talent competitions? You are sure of a good crowd, a lot of fun, and may well find acts you can use.

Coach parties

Forty or 50 people arriving for a drink or a snack can do wonders for a quiet lunch-time, and a regular coach trade can transform your turnover. You must be fully organised to accommodate and serve rapidly a sudden influx of large numbers, and you must consider the probable effect on your regular clientele. However, these potential problems can be largely alleviated by accepting coach parties by appointment only, and perhaps only taking those due to arrive at normally quiet times. Get on to the local and national bus companies and let them know of your willingness to accommodate them. And always look after the drivers. They are the ones who bring you the business.

Sidelines

Sidelines can become very profitable by using space and facilities outside opening hours which would otherwise be idle. Breakfast and afternoon teas may well be a needed service in your area. Business meetings and conferences bring in not only hire charges, but also sales of refreshments, meals and extra trade at opening time. Wedding receptions, club functions, Rotary, Round Table and Buffalo meetings, all provide similar opportunities.

Bed and breakfast
Bed and breakfast is a well-tried favourite, and with good reason. You are using facilities that are largely already financed by the pub side of the business, while usually bringing extra trade into the bars and restaurant.

Off-sales
Your off-sales department is open when all other shops are closed, and its overheads are almost non-existent. Make full use of it by selling cigarettes and confectionery as well as alcohol and soft drinks.

Success
However you see your future development, be sure to base it firmly on the foundation of your basic business policy and to harness your ambition and enthusiasm with total professionalism, allied to tight financial control. This is the path to success.

Appendix

Books

A Guide to Employment Law (National Union of Licensed Victuallers)

An ABC of Licensing Law (National Union of Licensed Victuallers)

An A-Z of Employment and Safety Law, Peter Chandler (Kogan Page)

Consumer Law for the Small Business, Patricia Clayton (Kogan Page)

Croner's Reference Book for the Self-employed and Smaller Business (Croner Publications)

Ergonomics, Functional Design for the Catering Industry, RHD Strank (Edward Arnold)

How to Buy a Business, Peter Farrell (Kogan Page)

Innkeeping (Brewing Publications Ltd, 42 Portman Square, London W1H 0BB)

Law for the Small Business, The Daily Telegraph Guide, Patricia Clayton (Kogan Page)

Pub Catering Operations (Brewing Publications Ltd, address above)

Running Your Own Wine Bar, Judy Ridgway (Kogan Page)

The Traditional English Pub, Ben Davis (Architectural Press)

Working for Yourself: The Daily Telegraph Guide to Self-employment, Godfrey Golzen (Kogan Page)

The World Atlas of Wine, Hugh Johnson (Mitchell Beazley)

Journals

Caterer & Hotelkeeper, Quadrant House, The Quadrant, Sutton, Surrey SM2 5AS

Catering and Hotel Management, Link House, Dingwell Avenue, Croydon, Surrey CR9 2AT

Free House, 5b Lower Market Arcade, Newcastle-under-Lyme, Staffordshire ST5 1QB

Free Trade Review, Sun Alliance and London House, Curzon Street, Derby

Innkeeping Today, Journal of the British Institute of Innkeeping, 42 Portman Square, London W1H 0BB

Licensee, Journal of the National Union of Licensed Victuallers, Boardman House, 2 Downing Street, Farnham, Surrey GU9 7NX

The Morning Advertiser, 57 Effra Road, London SW2

Pub Caterer, Quadrant House, The Quadrant, Sutton, Surrey SM2 5AS

The Publican, Maclaren House, 195 Scarbrook Road, Croydon, Surrey CR9 1QH

Courses

For information on licensed trade courses contact:
The British Institute of Innkeeping
42 Portman Square, London W1H 0BB; 01-486 4831

Useful addresses

Alliance of Small Firms and Self-Employed People
42 Vine Road, East Molesey, Surrey KT8 9LF; 01-979 2293

British Institute of Innkeeping
42 Portman Square, London W1H 0BB; 01-486 4831

British Insurance Brokers' Association
14 Bevis Marks, London EC3A 7NT; 01-623 9043

Campaign for Real Ale Ltd
34 Alma Road, St Albans, Hertfordshire AL1 3BW

Health and Safety Commission
Regina House, 259 Old Marylebone Road, London NW1 5RR; 01-723 1262

Health and Safety Executive
25 Chapel Street, London NW1 5DT; 01-262 3277
HM Customs and Excise
VAT Administration Directorate, King's Beam House, Mark Lane, London EC3R 7HE; 01-283 8911
National Association of Licensed House Managers
9 Coombe Lane, London SW20
National Union of Licensed Victuallers
Boardman House, 2 Downing Street, Farnham, Surrey GU9 7NX
Performing Rights Society Ltd
29 Berners Street, London W1A 4PP; 01-580 5544

Index

Accountant 24, 25, 29, 30, 33, 39, 41, 42, 105, 109, 110, 112

accounts 29, 30, 33, 40, 42, 105-14

advertising and publicity 34, 36, 41, 54-65, 78, 90, 94, 147, 149, 150

after-hours drinking 124-5, 127

alterations 28, 34, 123-8

amusement machines 22, 30, 130

Annual Licensing Meeting 124

appearance of pub:
  exterior 57-60
  interior 60-76

atmosphere 13, 14, 17, 18, 34, 40, 54, 62, 63, 64, 68, 72, 75, 102, 115, 120

Back shelves 71-2, 89, 90, 133, 135, 136, 138, 139

bank manager 24, 31, 35, 38, 40, 108-9

bar counter 28-9, 71-2, 118, 123, 138, 139

bar equipment 92-3, 94, 126

bars 61-3, 75-6

basic business policy 18-19, 31, 40, 44, 46, 51, 78, 88, 91, 115, 117, 127, 152

bed and breakfast 152

beer 22, 54, 59, 78-83, 90, 129, 139
  adulteration 131
  bottled 29, 82-3, 84
  cask-conditioned 78-81, 135
  dilution 131
  dispense 83
  keg 81-2, 135
  loss 111

measures 130-31
  pipe cleaning 82, 135
  real ale 78-81, 135
  refrigeration 79, 81, 82-3
  secondary fermentation 79, 82
  testing 80, 136

beer garden 25, 27, 28, 33, 59, 134, 146, 147, 149

betting 127, 129-30

blackboards 43, 58-9, 90, 136

book-keeping 21, 32, 107, 112, 133

bottle store 82, 135

bottling-up 135

brewers 12, 21, 22, 23, 25, 26, 38, 39, 40, 42, 91, 126

brewery loans 38-9

brewery ties 22, 23, 41

British Insurance Brokers' Association 114, 154

brokers 25, 26, 38, 39, 42

building societies 38

business name registration 42

buying:
  drinks 90-92
  food 95-6
  equipment 92-3, 102-3
  pub 41

Campaign for Real Ale 78, 154

capital 20, 22, 24, 34, 94, 149

car 34, 36

car-parking 27, 28, 29, 33, 59, 60, 123, 134, 138, 149

carpets 29, 70, 134

cash book 107, 108, 112, 113, 133

cash float 44, 106, 133

cash flow 34-8, 108-9
  projection 34, 36-7, 39, 41, 108-9, 111, 113, 147

156

Index

cashing up 106, 133
catering:
  condiments 97, 100
  desserts 98, 103
  dry goods 29
  equipment 29, 34, 35, 98,
    102-3
  frozen foods, 98, 99
  garnishes 99
  kitchen 29, 101, 102, 149
  menu 42, 94, 95, 97-8, 99,
    102
  orders 100-102
  portion control 101
  portions 96-7
  preparation 136
  refrigeration 29, 98-9, 103
  service 100
  supplies 95-6
  unpaid bills 102
cellar 29, 79, 81, 135-6, 138
  temperature 79
change 44
change-over day 42-5, 123
charity events 56-7
cheques 131
children 9, 26, 128-9, 143-4
children's room 33, 146, 147,
  149
cigarettes 22, 88-9, 129, 135,
  152
cleaning 133-5
  beer pipes 82, 135-6
  cellar 81-2, 135-6
  kitchen 104, 134-5, 138
clerk to the licensing
  justices 42, 124, 126, 127,
  128
closing time 137
coaches 151
cocktails 84, 87-8, 90, 150
cold shelf 82-3, 93, 135
competition 16, 29, 33, 40,
  147
complaints 49-50
conditions of service 112, 116
contract of employment 116-17
copyright 74, 131
counter 28, 29, 71-2, 118,
  123, 138, 139
credit 131
customers:
  loyalty 96, 141

  relations 44, 48-51, 129, 131
  service 119
  undesirable 51-3, 61
  wants and needs 46-8
Customs and Excise 42, 112;
  see also VAT

Dancing 127-8, 130
darts 33, 129, 149, 150
debts 131
decor 14, 18, 60, 61, 64-7,
  68, 75-6, 149
decoration 18, 21, 28, 29, 33,
  34, 63, 65-6, 68
discounts 92, 96
discrimination 116, 130
dispense 82, 83, 84-5, 117
draymen 44
drinking-up time 124
drunkenness 127, 129

Employees, *see* staff
employment legislation 112-13,
  116-17, 120-21, 129, 130
empties 135
entertainment 16, 33, 54, 131,
  148
    licence 127-8
entry into the trade 20-24
Environmental Health
  Officer 50, 104
expansion 149-52
extended hours order 128
extension of hours 123, 125

Family 8, 21
fidelity bond 20
finance 23, 24, 25, 31-9, 40,
  148
fire precautions 103, 127, 138
fires 73, 133, 136
flooring 70, 75-6
flowers 59, 66-7, 134, 136
food, *see* catering
free house 20, 21, 23, 41
friends 142, 143
  entertainment of 125
fuel 21, 35, 36, 43, 73, 94,
  124, 125, 133
function room 25, 148, 149
furniture 14, 18, 29, 34, 44,
  60, 61, 63, 67-70, 75-6,
  113, 133
future planning 18, 145-52

157

Games 30, 129-30, 149, 150
gaming 127, 129-30
glasses 83, 84, 86-7, 90, 117,
    118, 138
        government stamp 83,
            130, 131
        washers 93
goodwill 22, 23
gross profit 35, 94, 107, 109-11

Hand pumps 80
happy hour 150
health:
    personal 10, 33, 140, 142
    public, *see* Environmental
        Health Officer *and*
        hygiene
heating 29, 72-3, 137
holidays 9, 15, 117, 142-3,
    147, 148
hours of work 9, 10, 140
hygiene 83, 93, 100, 103-4,
    116, 117

Ice buckets 86
ice makers 93
industrial tribunal 116, 119,
    120
ingoings 34
Inland Revenue 42, 105, 113
insurance 21, 33, 34, 113-14
    brokers 114
    expenses 37
interest charges 24, 37, 39
interviews 39-41, 116
inventory 34, 44
invoices 107, 112, 133
    register 107, 109, 112, 133

Juke-box 59, 74

Keg beer 81-2
kitchen 29, 101, 102, 149;
    see also catering
        equipment 29, 34, 102-3

Landladies 11
landlord's personality 9-10,
    14-16, 17, 25, 28, 32, 33,
    40, 54, 61, 115, 119
law 9, 16, 52, 116, 120, 122-31
leasehold 20, 23-4
licences 43, 123-8
Licensed Victuallers'
    Association 25, 110-11, 126

licensing justices 42, 43, 128;
    see also magistrates
licensing law 16, 122-31, 137
lighting:
    emergency 127
    exterior 60, 137, 138
    interior 63-4, 71-2, 76, 89,
        90, 137
loans 21-3, 31-9, 42, 146
looking for a pub 25-7

Magistrates 43, 122, 123, 127,
    129; *see also* licensing
        justices
management 20, 21
marketing:
    drinks 39, 89-90
    food 96-100
market research 95
marriage 143
mealtimes 132
menu 42, 94, 95, 97-8, 99,
    102
microwave oven 98, 99, 136
minors 123, 127, 128-9
mixers 84, 85
Morning Advertiser 26
music 61, 73-5, 127-8, 131,
    150-51

National Insurance 42, 113
newspapers 25, 26, 54, 55, 56
notices 43, 67, 75, 87, 89-90,
    136
    legal 124, 130, 131

Occasional licences 123, 126
office organisation 42, 114
off-sales 71, 124, 152
opening hours 123, 124-5, 134,
    151
opening time 43, 132, 133, 137
optics 93, 131, 135, 137
overdraft 33, 38, 108, 109,
    119, 146
ownership 20, 23

Paperwork 114, 133, 137
partners 9-10, 143
PAYE 42, 105, 113
pension 23, 113
Performing Rights Society
    131, 155
personal life 143

Index

pilferage 88-9, 101, 107, 111, 134
planning 18, 94, 145-52
planning office 27, 29, 57
police 43, 53, 122-3, 124, 125, 126, 127, 128, 129
pool tables 22, 59, 150
popularity 9, 16, 45
press 25, 26, 142
price-lists 90, 131
prices:
   of pubs 20, 23, 34, 41, 42
   purchasing: drink 22, 23, 35, 91; equipment 93; food 95
   selling: drink 90, 91, 111; food 94, 95, 97
private accommodation 21, 25, 28, 33, 149
professional advice 24-5
professionalism 10, 16-18, 19, 24, 32, 39, 41, 44, 83, 87, 88, 91, 115, 117, 118, 142, 152
profitability 25, 30, 90, 105, 151
profit margin 22, 35, 88, 93, 94, 102, 109-11
promotions 92
property 23, 25-6, 33
protection order 43, 123
public holidays 92, 125, 126, 150
public liability insurance 113

Race relations 116, 130
radio 131
rates 21, 36
real ale 78-81
refrigeration 29, 81, 82, 93, 98-9, 103, 135
removal 43
   expenses 34
rent 21, 22, 23, 24
repairs 21, 22, 23, 34, 37
residents 125
restaurant 25, 33, 94, 131, 148, 149, 152
retirement 22-3
roof 28

Seasonal trade 26, 35
security 123, 137, 138, 141

security deposit 20, 34
service 93, 94, 100
sex discrimination 116, 130
sidelines 151
signs 30, 43, 57-9, 60, 89-90, 136, 146, 149
signing-in book 113
singing 127
snuff 65
soft drinks 22, 29, 88, 91, 152
   dispense 84
solicitor 24, 25, 38, 41, 43, 56
special events 56, 57, 150-51
special hours certificate 128
spirits 22, 29, 83-5, 91
   adulteration 131
   dilution 131
   dispense 84-5
   measures 130-31
staff 27, 35, 86, 94, 112, 115-21, 126, 129, 130, 140, 144, 147
   delegation 119-20, 141
   dismissal 9, 117, 120-21
   drinking 119
   engagement 115
   insurance 113
   misconduct 120
   notice 120
   references 116
   supervision 118-19
stillage 79, 80, 81
stock cards 42, 91, 109, 133
stock control 21
stock rotation 81, 82, 135
stocktaker 42, 43
stocktaking 91-2, 109-11
strategy 145-8
success 17, 19, 119, 152
supper licence 123, 127
survey 42

Tapping casks 79-80
targets 145, 146
tax 42, 105, 113
telephone 43
   expenses 36
television 131, 132, 144
temperature:
   of cellar 79
   of wine 86
tenancy 20, 21-3, 24, 26, 29, 77, 113, 126

159

negotiating for 39-41
theft 88-9, 101, 107-11, 134
tied houses 22, 24, 26, 34
till 44, 102, 106-7, 111, 113, 120, 138
tiltstick 81
time off 9, 120, 140-44
tobacco, *see* cigarettes
toilets 29, 33, 134, 136, 138
tourism 29, 30, 33, 56
Trading Standards Officer 130-31
training courses 77
transfer sessions 43, 123
trouble-makers 53, 123

Under-age drinking 123, 127, 128-9
unpaid bills 102

VAT 35, 37, 105, 107, 109, 112, 131
    registration 42, 112
venting 79

violence 52, 122, 129

Wages 35, 36, 106, 108, 112-13, 116, 125
    book 42, 113
    councils 112
    inspectorate 112
    statement 113-17
waste 98
water jugs 84, 135
wife 21, 144
wine 12, 22, 29, 85-7, 89, 91
    adulteration 131
    by the bottle 86
    by the glass 85-6, 90
    dilution 131
    glasses 86-7
    lists 86
    measures 130-31
    service 86
    temperature 86
    tasting 85, 136
working hours 9, 10